# LESSONS IN CREATIVITY

# LESSONS IN CREATIVITY

Stories and Strategies to
Cultivate Your **Creative Confidence**

# BEN RENNIE

WILEY

ISBN: 978-1-394-33113-0

 A catalogue record for this book is available from the National Library of Australia

*Registered Office*
John Wiley & Sons Australia, Ltd. Level 4, 600 Bourke Street, Melbourne, VIC 3000, Australia

For details of our global editorial offices, customer services, and more information about Wiley products visit us at www.wiley.com.

Wiley also publishes its books in a variety of electronic formats and by print-on-demand. Some content that appears in standard print versions of this book may not be available in other formats.

Trademarks: Wiley and the Wiley logo are trademarks or registered trademarks of John Wiley & Sons, Inc. and/or its affiliates in the United States and other countries and may not be used without written permission. All other trademarks are the property of their respective owners. John Wiley & Sons, Inc. is not associated with any product or vendor mentioned in this book.

*Limit of Liability/Disclaimer of Warranty*
While the publisher and author have used their best efforts in preparing this work, they make no representations or warranties with respect to the accuracy or completeness of the contents of this work and specifically disclaim all warranties, including without limitation any implied warranties of merchantability or fitness for a particular purpose. No warranty may be created or extended by sales representatives, written sales materials or promotional statements for this work. This work is sold with the understanding that the publisher is not engaged in rendering professional services. The advice and strategies contained herein may not be suitable for your situation. You should consult with a specialist where appropriate. The fact that an organisation, website, or product is referred to in this work as a citation and/or potential source of further information does not mean that the publisher and author endorse the information or services the organisation, website, or product may provide or recommendations it may make. Further, readers should be aware that websites listed in this work may have changed or disappeared between when this work was written and when it is read. Neither the publisher nor author shall be liable for any loss of profit or any other commercial damages, including but not limited to special, incidental, consequential, or other damages.

Cover Design by Wiley
Cover Concept and Background: Ben Rennie and Glenn Chandler
Cover Images: © Paper Trident/Getty Images; © hudiemm/Getty Images
Cover Photo: Ben Baker

Set in 10.5/12.5pt Utopia Std by Straive, Chennai, India
SKYB1AEBC61-C234-40EF-907E-1D50F72BB1D6_040925

*For my mum.*

# TABLE OF CONTENTS

## Part VI: Horizons: Growth — **169**

# FOREWORD

Let's talk about Ben for a moment. What does Ben actually do? That question has been thrown around in a few of our circles over the years, and it tells you a lot about him. The question doesn't indicate a nebulous approach to his work life, but instead reflects his creative approach to life in general.

Ben is eternally curious. Since I've known him, he's also been questioning how we approach work and life — and, more importantly, what brings us joy. Ben loves life and isn't afraid of change. He embraces it and charges at it full speed — he's not one for the comfort zone.

He's a contrarian in the best and most positive ways, undeniably charming, and authentically self-deprecating in the best possible way. He's full of contradictions and can sometimes seem like a hapless labrador, bouncing off walls, but he's also got a razor-sharp mind.

Well before I met him, he had long golden locks of hair and was one of the most promising cricketers in the country. In a sport-loving nation, this should have been the pinnacle for any young bloke — but not for Ben.

Despite his enviable skills (Mark Waugh once claimed he was the most naturally talented cricketer he'd ever seen), he gave it up to pursue unknown adventures. He knew there was more for him than standing in a field chasing a ball. The world was pulling him in a different direction.

That direction has had many twists and turns, which you'll read about in this exceptional book by a bloke who, in many ways, has been waiting for the future to catch up with where his head's at.

Ben inspires me, sometimes confuses me, but always makes me think about doing things differently. Creative people love to challenge the status quo and forge their own path.

I've learned a great deal from Ben over the years. I have marvelled at and been inspired by his relationship with his children and Nicola and their lives together — he always speaks of family first.

He's a bloke who was never meant to be stuck in the nets — his mind and spirit needed more than that.

So, what does he do? He's just Ben, full-time, and he's very good at his job.

**Tim Ross**
**Comedian, Writer and TV Presenter**

# ABOUT THE AUTHOR

In 2016, Ben Rennie took the ultimate leap of faith: he resigned from his company to start again, and build the company he had always wanted. Ben's business journey has been marked by failures, breakthroughs and the pursuit of ideas that matter. Today, Ben is the co-founder and managing partner of Reny®, a Certified B Corporation dedicated to climate design, clean creative and systemic innovation. At the heart of his work lies Orbital Design, a philosophy that reimagines the role of design by giving Mother Nature a seat at the table, balancing human needs with the systems we inhabit.

While challenges and triumphs have marked Ben's professional journey, his most meaningful creative endeavour has been raising his three children. To him, parenting is a deeply creative act — instilling in his kids the courage to embrace their creative confidence, take risks and trust in their ideas and abilities is nothing short of transformative.

Ben champions the power of creative confidence, applying it to some of the world's most iconic brands — including Patagonia, Nike, John Holland, Westpac and Canon. Whether collaborating with these industry leaders or speaking on global stages such as TEDx and Vivid Sydney, his mission is unwavering: to inspire and empower people to tackle the world's most pressing challenges through creativity and meaningful connection.

His journey has taken him from the beaches of Stanwell Park in Australia, where he lives with his family, to the deserts of Utah and the vibrant landscapes of Salt Lake City, where he has lived on and off for the past five years. These contrasting environments have profoundly shaped his perspective and the understanding that creativity flourishes when we protect nature, embrace failure, adapt our ideas, nurture relationships and cultivate our creative confidence.

*Lessons in Creativity* is the culmination of Ben's work and reflections — a guide to reigniting the power of imagination and using it to craft a more sustainable and inspired future, driven by the limitless potential of creative confidence.

# PREFACE

Creativity is one of the most powerful forces we possess. It shapes how we understand the world, solve problems and build the future. It's what we use to overcome challenges, shape our lives, spark innovation and improve things. But somewhere along the way, many of us lose touch with it. According to Adobe's 2012 'State of Create' global study, as kids, 96 per cent of us believe we're creative — everything feels possible. By adulthood, that number plummets to just 26 per cent. I call this the *creativity gap*, and it's not just a statistic — it's an emergency. Because creativity isn't exclusive to artists or designers; it's for everyone.

And that's precisely why I wrote this book.

For years, I worked within the human-centred design (HCD) framework — a process that puts people at the heart of problem-solving. And this framework did me and my colleagues a lot of good. It taught us to listen, empathise and create with the user in mind. But, as time went on, HCD started to feel incomplete. Yes, we were solving problems for people, but we weren't seeing the whole picture. We weren't thinking about the systems we were impacting — including the climate, the environment, communities, the future and our neighbours. I realised we were designing solutions that offered immediate convenience for humans but created long-term inconveniences for humanity — similar to the issues connected with single-use plastics. These solutions provide a quick fix for today but leave irreparable consequences for the planet.

Everything around us was once an idea. Every object, every solution we interact with, was designed by someone, probably starting with a pencil and some paper. And here is what 19 years as a designer has taught me: every endpoint, where the last person left off, is a new beginning. We don't need to reinvent the world from scratch; we just need to pick up where the past left off. This is the beauty of creativity — reimagining, redesigning and recreating. Ideas evolve continuously, and each new perspective pushes us forward; each endpoint, a new beginning. Embracing this is known as having *creative confidence*. An idea championed by Tim Brown of IDEO, this is the ability to believe in our innate (always been inside of us) ability to dive in and solve problems.

After years in the design and creative industries, I realised that design and HCD needed rethinking. So, I created systemic design foundations (SDF). SDF, also named, orbital design, takes a more holistic approach—it's about considering the human need *and* the ripple effects of every design decision. It's a way to understand the systems we operate in and design with people and the planet in mind. Creativity isn't just about making things better for us today—it's about leaving things better for those who come after us.

Orbital design is my life's work—a way to challenge the traditional models of design and broaden the scope of how we view creativity. Through my work with brands such as Patagonia, Surfrider Foundation, B Corp, 1% for the Planet, Tourism Australia, Chanel, Oakley and the Indigenous Marathon Foundation, I've seen firsthand the impact this approach can have. It's about intention, foresight and the understanding that what we create today will send ripples into the future. This is also relevant to our personal lives, influencing how we live and the choices we make.

This book is a reflection of my journey. It's predominately a collection of stories — highlighting moments in my life and career when creativity sparked something bigger. These stories, and the lessons I learned from them and the people I met, show that creativity isn't reserved for 'geniuses' or 'visionaries'. It's for all of us — anyone willing to see things differently and leap with creative confidence to start something new.

The tales I include through this book are usually reserved for late nights with old friends, swapping war stories over good wine. But I share them here — the wins, the losses, the failures, the lies and the truths — in the hope that they inspire you to rethink, reframe and even reset. I also reveal lessons learned from the world's best brands, sharing the wisdom usually locked away in boardrooms.

This book is divided into six parts, each representing a stage in the creative process reimagined through the lens of my life and how I approach it, based on what I have learned about creativity. This book is designed to awaken your creative confidence to reframe how your thinking and presence are directly responsible for reshaping the world. When seen through the lenses of awareness, purpose, resilience and mastery, creativity becomes the key to tackling today's most pressing challenges — from climate change to social justice to redefining what it means to live well (or start over again, if that is what you crave).

As you read this book, I hope you see yourself in these stories. I hope you rediscover the creativity you may have set aside or forgotten. Most importantly, I want you to realise that creativity isn't something you either have or don't have — it's a way of thinking, a way of approaching the world with curiosity and a belief that things can always be better.

This isn't just a book about creativity — it's about creative confidence. And that's something we all have within us. The fact that you're holding this book means you're already on that path.

Let's get started.

# INTRODUCTION: ESCAPE

As author and international advisor on education in the arts Sir Ken Robinson once pointed out, 'The problem isn't that we aim too high and fail — it's just the opposite — we aim too low and succeed'. This truth lies at the heart of the creativity gap between the kids who think they're creative, and those who think the same thing as adults. Too often, we stop stretching our imaginations, settling for what's easily within reach instead of pushing the boundaries of possibility. But creativity demands more. Sometimes, it asks us to be brave; other times, it requires patience. Yet, at its core, creativity, much like when we were children, encourages us to dream. It pushes us to take risks, to imagine more and to believe in what might be.

I'm obsessed with creative confidence — that belief in our innate creativity. It took me decades to find mine. Without it, this book wouldn't exist. But it wasn't an easy journey. Only after countless failures did I realise, despite those missteps, I was still okay. I was still intact. Creative confidence is about believing in your ability to make a difference in the world — or the world around you — and understanding your place. It's not about coming up with one genius idea that solves everything; it's about trying — and failing — through hundreds of attempts until you arrive at the place you always envisioned (or the product you dreamed of creating). It requires us to dream bigger, take risks and challenge ourselves to aim higher — not just for our benefit, but also for our impact on the world and the people we share it with. For me, that's my wife, Nicola, and our three kids: Miff, 21; Kai, 18 and Pip, 15. You will meet them all a little later.

Crucible moments are those pivotal points in life that, on reflection, set us on a new path toward becoming who we've always aspired to be. To set the tone for the chapters of this book, I want to start with my crucible moment — a moment that changed everything. You might see it as a failure or perhaps as a day of enlightenment. Maybe this kind of moment is typical for you. But, for me, it was the day that shifted everything — and redefined the rest of my life.

**Crucible moments are those pivotal points in life that, on reflection, set us on a new path toward becoming who we've always aspired to be.**

It was late November 2016; I was in McLaren Vale, a wine region just south of Adelaide, working with one of Australia's largest banks and on the verge of wrapping up another successful project. That morning, however, the vineyards, usually a symbol of growth and prosperity, seemed shrouded in an ethereal mist, reflecting the uncertainty clouding my mind. This meeting felt different, weighted with the culmination of years of dedication and relentless effort coming to a breaking point. The crisp morning air did little to ease the knot in my stomach. All I could think about was the growing dissonance between my current reality and the vision I had once created.

I had a habit of arriving 30 minutes early to meetings, a routine that allowed me to let the nerves settle and plan my approach. Maybe the feeling gnawing at me was simply the pressure after six months of relentless work on this project with one of Australia's largest banks. Maybe not. I parked the car and took a moment to breathe the morning air. The boardroom was in a small, rustic building nestled among the vineyards. The contrast between the natural beauty outside and the corporate atmosphere inside was stark. The crunching sound underfoot was oddly comforting as I walked up the gravel path. I paused at the door, looking back at the misty vineyards one last time before stepping inside.

For the seven years leading up to that morning in McLaren Vale, I had been on a deeply personal journey building my company, 6.2, an innovation lab. The name 6.2 is not just a random combination of numbers; it reflects my birthday, 6 February. As a creative person, naming things, oddly, has always been a challenge for me, but 6.2 felt right; it was personal and represented a part of me. I co-founded 6.2 with Paul Breen (aka 'The Bull'), a Melbourne entrepreneur famous for his balanced ethics, passion for business, loyalty and ferocious (but fair) approach. We created an innovation consultancy designed to push boundaries and solve complex problems.

The early days were a struggle, filled with uncertainty and unrelenting effort. Paul and I operated from different cities — Paul in Melbourne and myself in Sydney. We faced a steep learning curve, spending countless hours pitching our vision to anyone who would listen. Rejection became a familiar companion, but each 'no' only fuelled our determination.

Slowly, our persistence began to pay off, and word began to spread about our work. We hustled, networked and showcased our work at every opportunity. Each project was a stepping stone, and we took immense pride in the relationships we built and the solutions we delivered.

As our reputation took root, we found ourselves in the boardrooms of Australia's most prominent companies: Australia Post, Westpac, Gulf Oil, the City of Sydney, Tourism Australia and global icons such as Nike and Adidas. We were slowly acquiring market share from the world's best consultancies, such as McKinsey, IDEO, PwC and Capgemini. Each success was a testament to the hard work and sleepless nights we had invested. Many early mornings, late insights and months without a salary gave way to opportunity and scale. Each project allowed us to prove ourselves and bring fresh perspectives and innovative solutions. We weren't just solving problems; we were reimagining possibilities — and developing insights that now fill the pages of this book.

Building 6.2 was about more than big clients and high-profile projects, however. We wanted to push the boundaries and show it was possible to solve complex problems with creativity and innovation. Our mission was clear: make unremarkable businesses remarkable and fight for the small businesses. The journey was extraordinary, filled with extreme highs and extreme lows.

And for a while, it felt like we were succeeding. Our approach to problem-solving was unique, and our ability to deliver results earned us a solid reputation. We believed in what we were building.

By 2012, I was receiving all kinds of invitations to speak to magazines, TV and events on 6.2 and my role as an innovation leader. I was invited to give a TEDx talk to address the federal government on design thinking at Parliament House, where I had the unique opportunity to present to the prime minister. I spoke at Vivid Sydney, Creative Sydney, City of Melbourne, Denmark House, in Fiji, Hamilton Island, the Gold Coast and Perth, and at trade shows in the United States. I was busy — all affirmations of our hard work and vision. I commanded fees of up to five figures for speaking engagements, sharing our journey and insights with audiences hungry for inspiration and innovation.

The years between 2009 and 2013 were a blur of relentless drive and crucible moments. I am immensely proud of the work and the stories from that era. These experiences have shaped the course of my professional life.

However, as we grew, a dissonance began to creep in; I could sense an unsettling undercurrent. What had started as a purpose-driven venture became a source of internal conflict. I was spending more and more time away from my family, living out of a suitcase and constantly on the road. Each trip took me further from the life I had pictured and the people I created it for.

The business took a lot of work to scale, and I struggled to extricate myself from the daily grind. Despite our success, I felt trapped in relentless work and perpetual motion. 6.2's original mission was noble. Yet, the more we grew, the further I felt we strayed from it. Our clients were now the very corporate giants I had left behind in search of the businesses that needed us. Now, we had no time for them. We had become advisors to the elite.

A growing disillusionment overshadowed the excitement of securing big contracts. I found myself questioning the impact of our work. Were we making a difference or simply another cog in the machine? A gnawing sense of unease replaced the drive and dedication that had fuelled 6.2's early days.

I remember sitting in countless boardrooms and feeling a profound disconnect between the corporate environment and my values. The hustle and grind, once exhilarating, now felt suffocating. The irony was stark: in our quest to innovate and disrupt, we had become enmeshed in the system we had set out to transform.

## INSIGHTS

Any service in any industry will naturally attract a specific clientele, with specific expectations and behavioural traits. As entrepreneur and bestselling author Seth Godin states, 'Choose your customers, choose your future'. When you understand this, you're not just meeting but also strategically engaging with the inherent features — or challenges — that come with your chosen sector. We had picked our customers, and this had set us on the wrong path.

We all have a place that grounds us and makes us feel at ease. Everything seems to settle down, and we can think clearly and patiently. For me, that place has always been in nature; the ocean or mountains are my safe places.

As I held the door to the boardroom that morning, I glanced back at the vineyards in McLaren Vale and I was transported back to a time when life felt more connected and grounded. The mist that clung to the vines took me back to the crisp, cold air of the Australian Alps when my wife, Nicola, and I were volunteer ski patrollers at Mt Selwyn between 2006 and 2012.

The mornings on the mountain were nothing short of magical. We would wake before dawn, arrive at the resort at 6 am, bundle up against the chill and prepare the mountain for a new day. I would head out on the Ski-doo snowmobile, the engine's hum breaking the morning silence as I checked the lifts, roped off the resort boundaries and marked hazards. The world was still asleep, and the mountain was ours alone.

As I reached the resort's edge, I would cut the motor on the Ski-doo and stand there in silence, my breath hanging in the cold air. There's something profoundly peaceful about being in nature, on the top of a mountain, with nothing but the sound of the wind and the snow crunching underfoot. The vast expanse of white, the clear blue sky and the untouched snow created a feeling of serenity and purpose. It was a stark contrast to the boardrooms and business meetings that now filled my days, a world away from the corporate grind and the constant hustle.

Those moments on the mountain were grounding. They reminded me of the simplicity of hard work and the deep connection to nature and purpose. In nature, I felt a profound sense of fulfilment, an increasingly elusive clarity in my current life. The mornings spent at Mt Selwyn were a reminder of what truly mattered: the quiet moments, the connection to the natural world and the sense of doing something meaningful and tangible.

Now, surrounded by the rolling vineyards of McLaren Vale, I longed for that simplicity and peace. I opened the door to the boardroom and walked inside. The weight of the impending meeting pressed down on me, a stark reminder of how far I had strayed from that path. The contrast was overwhelming; the vineyard's beauty and tranquillity were worlds apart from the sterile, high-pressure environment I was about to enter.

As the meeting began, a wave of anxiety washed over me. A knot tightened in my stomach as I felt almost angry at myself for leading us here. The room was filled with some of Australia's leading bank executives, and the energy was thick with anticipation.

As the discussion continued, I could feel my mind drifting. I excused myself and headed to the bathroom, hoping to collect my thoughts. I recalled a comment from comedian Jerry Seinfeld that when things weren't going well on set, he would splash his face with water to change his mood. Desperate for a reset, I tried it. The cold water hit my face, but nothing changed. The anxiety clung to me, unshakable.

I splashed my face again and again, but still — nothing. All I wanted was to be somewhere else, anywhere but there! The question kept echoing: if not here, then where? I felt trapped, suffocated by the environment I had worked so hard to create. The irony was bitter. Again, if not here, then where?

I paced the bathroom, staring into the mirror, trying to convince myself everything was okay. But deep down, I knew it wasn't. I had built a business reflecting everything I had sought to escape from in corporate Australia.

I took a deep breath, unbuttoned the top button on my shirt and walked back into the boardroom. I thanked everyone for their time and wished them success with the project. Then I left.

But I didn't just leave the room; I left the life I had created.

I drove straight to the airport, my mind racing with one thought: start again!

The next day, I resigned from my own company.

Within eight days, my family and I were on a flight to San Francisco. As the plane touched down in the United States, one thing was clear: I was on a path — maybe not even the right one, but it was a new one. Over the coming four years, this path lead me back to nature, to the mountains, the oceans and, most importantly, my family and the person I always wanted to be.

# PART I

# ORIGINS: FROM EMPATHY TO AWARENESS

Where creativity begins, with a new awareness of the world's complexities and the spark of possibilities

Creativity begins with awareness. I've learned that seeing the world differently is the first step to building creative confidence. It's about being open to what's happening around you—the challenges, the opportunities and the connections. The more aware you are, the clearer it becomes that creativity isn't just a skill—it's a way of seeing and responding to the world. It's a tool for making sense of complexity and a spark for meaningful change.

# CHAPTER 1

# SUPER UNKNOWN

Realising creativity lives in the unknown

The unrelenting sun showed no mercy as it descended. I stood there, trapped in a swirl of exhaustion and anxiety, frozen in place. Beads of sweat formed on my forehead—a testament to my nerves and the relentless heat. *Breathe*, I reminded myself, trying to calm my racing thoughts. I hadn't fully prepared for this moment but, somehow, I had convinced myself I was ready.

My heart raced as I closed my eyes, searching for strength. 'Visualise, be strong,' I whispered. Time felt elastic, stretching unbearably, but the buzz of the surrounding crowd snapped me back to reality. It was my turn, yet my feet were glued to the ground. I stood frozen.

In December 2006, I was 31, working for a great company with a great job. On paper, everything looked right. Yet, I found myself creatively stifled by the monotony of routine. The joy of fatherhood with my three-year-old daughter, Mia (Miff), was undeniable, and the prospect of another child, Kai, filled me with excitement. But in my work, I was stuck. I knew I needed something to shake me free from the rut. This was my way of breaking out—a leap into the unknown.

Growing up, Mum constantly reminded me that fear and opportunity go hand in hand. I recall her saying the only real way to know if we can fly is to leap (if anything, you will get good at landing)! My parents, always optimistic and encouraging, pushed me to find the courage to take leaps. So, with newfound resolve, I took a deep breath, leaned forward and took the leap.

Then—nothing. Darkness. Pure silence and darkness. Slowly, that darkness flirted with the edges of my vision before reluctantly retreating. I heard laughter and grumbles. Pain surged through my body. I reached for my side and opened my eyes to see two young schoolgirls standing over me, their eyes wide with a mixture of astonishment and concern, giggling.

'Are you okay, mister? That was insane!' exclaimed the older one.

I did a quick self-check — nothing seemed to be broken. I looked up at the younger girl, who seemed worried and amused, and managed an awkward smile. 'What were you doing up there, mister? That was crazy!'

I was asking myself the same thing: What was I doing up there?

At 31, with no recent experience, I had dropped into a 10-foot skate ramp at Monster Skate Park in Sydney. That darkness was caused by me, knocked out at the bottom of a skate ramp. At the time, my choice made sense; looking back, it seems nonsensical. But it happened.

I waved off an older man's offer to help, determined to regain my composure. 'Young man, I'm not sure if that was your first or last time, but it looked like you were diving into a swimming pool rather than a skate ramp,' he remarked.

I now know what drove me up that ramp: a deep yearning for a reset. Rest assured, I found a better way. And that better way is encapsulated in a single word: creativity. Creativity is the answer to most of our problems.

Designer and architect Charles Eames said, 'It is not easy to do something good, but it is extremely difficult to do something bad.' This reminds us that true creativity isn't easy — it requires both courage and persistence to create something meaningful. However, creative confidence is built when you take action, even when the path is unclear. Confidence comes from developing the resilience to keep moving forward, trusting that you'll eventually find your way through experimentation, failure and discovery.

> **True creativity isn't easy — it requires both courage and persistence to create something meaningful.**

The hardest part of any creative journey isn't just stepping into the unknown — it's believing in your ability to navigate that uncertainty. It's about trusting that even when you don't know how things will turn out, you're still willing to take that first step.

The same thing that drove me up that skate ramp would later give me the courage to resign from my successful company, 6.2, while married with three kids, to chase snow with my family.

◊◊◊

When we landed in the United States in 2016, eight days after walking out on not only that meeting in McLaren Vale but also my own company, we set up a plan. We flipped the script — from the office to the mountains. We went from our beachside town in Stanwell Park, my Sydney studio and three kids in school to leaving it all behind to find nature and some balance. I was 41.

Our plan was to spend three months in Lake Tahoe, California, right at the bottom of Heavenly Mountain. We would take some time out and hit reset. Those three months became four years. Over those four years, our family of five travelled the world chasing snow while designing, creating and eventually running a successful micro-creative agency from some of the most beautiful places on the planet.

# INSIGHTS

Leaving my business behind, which I had spent five years building, was terrifying. We needed everything to fall into place perfectly to afford to globe-trot around the world's best ski resorts. I must be clear: we couldn't afford to do this, but I couldn't afford not to. If things didn't fall into place, we could lose everything.

For four years, we flipped the switch on society's idea of normal. While our kids were still young enough to hang with us but old enough to understand the significance, we bounced between Stanwell Park in New South Wales, Australia, the mountains of California, Colorado, Salt Lake City and the cities of San Francisco, Los Angeles — with side trips to Italy, the United Kingdom, New Zealand and mountains in Australia. We chased winters relentlessly between 2016 and 2020, refining our understanding of nature, climate and intention, and building a company on the values of those experiences.

As I mention in the introduction, that meeting in late 2016 was a crucible moment for me. Now, I need to go back even further to introduce you to a few important people in this story. The rock who makes my world tick and who supported the crazy idea of leaving our world behind was my best friend and partner for life, Nicola Carter. I met Nicola in 1997. Nicola was on an adventure of her own, and our worlds collided in Sydney. Our first kiss was on a North Sydney train station platform. It wasn't just a moment in time that, for me at least, was the beginning of my life as I know it today. Our shared passions — adventure, nature, sports and snow — bound us. Nicola, a lawyer in the making, put her career on hold for the same reason I left cricket (I will get to cricket later): the pursuit of adventure.

Falling in love was the easiest thing I have ever done. We had shared a love of snow sports and the outdoors; adventure would be our guide. Nicola became my rock and muse, supporting my wildest dreams and half-baked ideas with unwavering enthusiasm. Even after over two decades together, she still listens to my crazy schemes, not with doubt but with the belief that each one is possible, that every half-baked plan could change everything — another new adventure.

Nicola is a life-altering connection who inspires me every day. I knew then, and I certainly know now, that the most critical decision we ever make is not where we work or who we party with but who we choose to build relationships with for the rest of our lives. Having a tribe you care for and love and who are also good teammates softens the rough edges and magnifies the shine of life. No decision in my life has been more critical.

Meeting Nicola in 1997 encapsulated the nineties for me, a decade that holds a special place in my heart; I adored that decade! It was an era of boundless optimism, untamed ambition and the belief that love could conquer all, marked by grunge music, iconic films and a cultural shift in sports like snowboarding and surfing, not to mention the internet. The decade promised a future more connected than we could have imagined, reshaping the world to the sounds of Pearl Jam, Nirvana, Hole and the Red Hot Chili Peppers. It is an unforgettable soundtrack to a decade filled with radical changes.

In 1998, Vancouver became my playground, and Nicola — who I would go on to marry in 2003 — became my true north. I was a 23-year-old Australian transitioning from cricket to snowy slopes, eager to discover a fresh path. Armed with a snowboard instructor certification, I found a new home among the mountains and immersed myself in this world: teaching, revelling in the nightlife, embarking on adventures and, most significantly, falling in love.

As we moved into 1999, I was on a mission to create my immortality through branding. However, building new brands proved challenging, so I sought partnerships with US brands looking for a foothold in Australia. I met several now-iconic brands, including meeting with eyewear brand VonZipper in Los Angeles before their official launch. Their wild, unconventional vibe made me sceptical about their business prospects. I also had breakfast with the founders of lifestyle brand Volcom, whose laid-back approach didn't strike me as a formula for success. Another meeting was with Sector 9 skateboards, where I wondered about the potential of those young entrepreneurs. A chance encounter with Merrell footwear ended in a pass from me. Interestingly, Adidas saw potential where I didn't, and, of course, VonZipper, Volcom and Sector 9 all saw significant success.

## INSIGHTS

At 24, I knew very little about the intricacies of business—while I had an undeniable desire to be part of it, I lacked any substantial knowledge. Potential lies not only in the idea behind a brand but also in its ability to solve a market problem, fill a gap and be driven by talented individuals. While market influencers contributed to the success of brands such as VonZipper, most success stories stem from a powerful vision, visionary leadership and a great team. It took me a long time to learn that lesson.

By 2000, I'd found the first company I wanted to align myself with—a small business called Utopia Optics. What followed was an extraordinary business journey where I built a lifelong admiration for part-owner Brad Gerlach, a legendary pro surfer and an icon out of California. Brad became crucial in my journey, introducing me to influential personalities such as Pamela Anderson, Snoop Dogg and Kelly Slater in Los Angeles. These encounters broadened my perspective and opened doors I never imagined. We created a fun, market-shifting brand that led to unforgettable experiences. In 2000, for example, we hosted Australia's first-ever Night Pipe Jam at Perisher Valley, an event built from scratch to showcase the country's rising snowboarding talent, including the then 13-year-old Torah Bright (now an Olympic gold and silver medallist and a family friend). We lit up the halfpipe with cherry pickers, creating a spectacle. Chris Mater from Red Bull backed the event, making it one of Red Bull's first partnerships in Australia.

In 2000, we also became the primary sponsor for the fifth year of the Offshore Festival, held at the same time as famous surfing competition in Bells Beach, Torquay (now known as the Rip Curl Pro). We rented a little beachside cabin and, by chance, shared it with Mick Fanning's family. That was the year the wiry 19-year-old Mick, as a wildcard, was invited to Bells for the first time at the beginning of his career, symbolising new hope for Australian surfing. He would go on to win it the following year.

We also learnt a lesson in what not to do. We handed out hundreds of Utopia Optics stickers, only to have people plaster them all over Bells. This led to a warning from the Torquay Council on environmental laws and the World Surf League threatening to ban us from the overuse of stickers at a significantly sponsored event. The lessons and experiences were hard and fast.

Those early years were a nonstop hustle, sustained by petrol fumes and relentless grit. You often don't orchestrate a culture; it happens organically. Our unplanned culture needed an astronomical jolt of energy. We'd haphazardly gained new brands such as LINE Skis, Onetrack Snowboards and Roial Clothing — all unproven start-ups. These were exciting propositions, but we needed the established legacy to catapult real growth.

One pivotal encounter during these years was with Chip Wilson, the visionary behind Westbeach (snow and surf apparel) and later Lululemon (premium athletic apparel). Chip's ability to capture and transform cultural trends into unique products was unmatched. I remember one meeting where he mentioned his new idea of athletic wear tailored for women. I dismissed it as uninspiring. In hindsight, it was a glimpse of a potential life-altering brand. At the time of writing, Lululemon Athletica was valued at over $40 billion.

These early lessons all fed into my creativity and approach when forming my company 6.2 in 2009. In some small way, they also fed into my decision to leave that company in 2016.

## INSIGHTS

Some people look at my decision to give up my company 6.2 to chase snow with my family at 41 and slap a 'mid-life crisis' label on it. That's lazy thinking. A crisis is a mess; what I did was calculated. It was based on years of understanding myself, my family and my business, and making a decision that aligned with all three.

Spending four years on the slopes isn't everyone's idea of 'normal', but who cares? I wasn't chasing normal; I wanted to blend my life by spending less time in meetings and dealing with red tape, and more time with my kids in nature. That's my version of being present: in the places I love, with the people I love.

Why do it? The answer is simple but not simplistic: clarity over certainty. I don't have all the answers, but I don't need to. Tossing out the old map, switching on real-time navigation and seeing where life leads is okay. This wasn't a hiccup or mistake but a deliberate recalibration. It was making a move—because standing still is the riskiest move of all!

So, don't call it a crisis. Call it a strategy. And I'd recommend it to anyone who questions the so-called given routes in life.

Travelling the world for four years in my early 40s certainly came with challenges. Some people assume I was aiming to give my kids an edge in snow sports to set them on a path to professional success. (I've even overheard parents telling friends I'm an ambitious father who wanted my kids to be world champions.) These are lovely side effects, but the reality was far more profound than that. It wasn't just about me, and it wasn't about my kids. It was about all of us: me, my wife and my kids, in that order. At some point, we all crave a reset. Most people fantasise about some sort of course correction in the shower or during the commute home, and then file it under 'unrealistic'. I turned my daydream into my daily life, but not on a whim. I turned the lens inward, weighed the trade-offs and consciously disrupted the comfort of the every day for the promise of something greater. This 'reset' wasn't spontaneous; it was a culmination of life events and professional milestones.

Nicola and I recognised that our path, while outwardly impressive, needed to be aligned with our inward values. My business no longer worked for me, and continuing down that road would do a disservice to me and my family.

What do you do when you've climbed the ladder only to find it's leaning against the wrong wall? You come down and find the right one. So I did. I took four years to roam the earth with my family, putting face time with my kids first. I reversed everything. I didn't ask how I could find the time to be present for my kids' sports; I wondered how I find the time to work after kids' sports. The dinner table took priority over late-night work, and standing on the knuckles of a jump to watch and support my kids' dreams became the priority.

**What do you do when you've climbed the ladder only to find it's leaning against the wrong wall? You come down and find the right one.**

I survived by foraging for work, like a hunter-gatherer, creating solutions for brands, advising, designing and helping from the road. I collaborated with small brands and big brands — and it worked. After four years of chasing snow and teaching my kids to land safely on 70-foot jumps (while skiing and snowboarding, to clarify), I found my own feet, my own safe landing. In 2022, I leaned into a refined venture, a new version of 6.2 — one that would allow me to be more hands-on creatively while staying committed to problem-solving, and one that would let me be exactly who I wanted to be and create a legacy that aligns with my values.

# INSIGHTS

Busy is all too commonly mistaken for purpose, as we're swept up in the relentless current of daily demands. But a whisper is within us all, a quiet call to something more genuine, more 'you'. This whisper is hidden in that subtle discomfort, that faint longing. For me, listening to that whisper is perhaps the most sincere conversation you'll ever have about the life you're meant to live. So, listen to that voice, the creative one, still inside of you that somehow, somewhere, back there, feels like it was left behind for something more secure.

You may not need to upend everything, but you may need to realign with your unique inner compass. These minor, meaningful adjustments bring you closer to a life that is not passively inherited but crafted with intention.

Remember — we all have the power to redesign our lives and the environments we inhabit. It's about making intentional choices, prioritising what matters, and being willing to challenge the status quo. You can shape your future through thoughtful design, whether in your personal life or in the broader world.

My experiences leading up to and through my four years chasing the snow gave me a profound understanding of creativity and its true importance. They underscored my role as a designer — creating better client products and designing my life. Four years of travelling and living immersed in nature gave me the clarity to delve deeper into the essence of design, and the role and importance of creativity. It pushed me to explore the complexities of human behaviour and the critical role design plays in shaping our future.

Creativity doesn't confine itself to an office's walls or a project's boundaries. It's a mindset, a way of approaching life that embraces the unknown, takes risks and evolves continuously. As a designer, I realised my work wasn't just about aesthetics or functionality, but about crafting meaningful experiences that push the world forward.

**Creativity is a mindset, a way of approaching life that embraces the unknown, takes risks and evolves continuously.**

Perhaps it's time to reconsider the 'follow your passion' mantra. Passion alone doesn't lead to success. Those already on the podium often romanticise it, reflecting on their achievements. But behind every success are failed ventures, pivots and hard choices. They knew when to adapt. Passion didn't carry them to the top — persistence and skill did.

Instead of chasing an elusive passion, focus on what you're good at and commit to improving. Put in the hours — 10 000 if you're counting. Excellence doesn't follow passion; it follows persistence. Your work and your dedication are what will shape your journey toward mastery.

Use your work and your life to make a positive impact. Mastery isn't just about getting better at what you do; it's about shaping the narrative of your life. Your stress and expectations all contribute to your story, shaped by your choices, effort and, ultimately, your creativity.

Design improves our lives in the present; creativity charts the path into the future. This idea has been the lens through which I've viewed problems and possibilities for over a decade — often seeing them as two sides of the same coin.

## INSIGHTS

Creativity isn't about having every answer from the start; it's about moving forward even when the path ahead is uncertain. Building creative confidence involves embracing the unknown and letting yourself learn as you go. Imagine your creative process to be like an adventure — don't stress about figuring out the whole journey at once; just keep your focus on taking the next step. The unknown isn't a source of fear; it's where the real magic happens.

So, take that leap, trust in yourself and let curiosity light the way forward.

# CHAPTER 2

# CRICKET FOR DUMMIES

Noticing the world in ways you haven't before

Dame Zaha Hadid, one of the world's most groundbreaking architects, was known for pushing the boundaries of design. Her work challenged conventions, bending space and form in ways that redefined modern architecture. Hadid's designs were bold, fluid and unrestrained, embodying her philosophy that creativity should never be confined to a single path. She believed in exploring every angle, every possibility — a philosophy that is summed up in her iconic quote: 'There are 360 degrees, so why stick to one?'

Hadid reminds us that creativity is expansive. It's about moving beyond the narrow confines of a single perspective or idea. Creativity, like design, can take any direction. Sticking to one approach limits our potential, while embracing the full range of possibilities opens up new paths. Creativity thrives when we allow it to move in any direction, influenced by the spaces we inhabit and the people we surround ourselves with. This is why your environment matters — it shapes how you think, see and allow your creativity to stretch. Whether it's the workplace, a cafe or even a casual gathering, every environment influences our ideas in ways we may not immediately recognise. The key is knowing how to curate those surroundings to unlock your creative potential.

Sometimes, places we visit transform our thinking, taking us back to somewhere old or inspiring us to think of something possible. This realisation hit me hard during a catch-up with the family at Hawke's Brewing. The energy of the place, the people and the shared passion created a spark in ways I hadn't anticipated.

Stepping into Hawke's Brewing in Sydney felt like being transported back to a classic Aussie bar from the 1980s. The brewery, a tribute to Australia's beloved Prime Minister Bob Hawke, was brimming with nostalgic charm. Hawke wasn't just a political icon; he was also the man who once held the world record for sculling a yard (1.4 litres) of ale — a feat that solidified his everyman appeal. The brewery's decor struck a perfect balance of retro and rustic, with weathered timber floors, exposed brick walls and vintage beer posters.

Nestled within this vibrant setting was the Lucky Prawn, a Chinese restaurant that captured the essence of old-school Australian Chinese cuisine — a staple across the country. As I sat down for a meal with my family, I couldn't help but marvel at the meticulous detail that went into crafting this authentic experience. The space itself — its history, energy and atmosphere — was an integral part of the creativity that seemed to flow effortlessly.

The red marbled carpet, paper lanterns and familiar aroma of soy sauce and ginger instantly transported me back to my childhood, when my uncles Tom and Gus (Mum's older brothers) had purchased the Narrandera Hotel in western New South Wales. Narrandera, a sleepy town on the banks of the Murrumbidgee River, six hours west of Sydney, was where everyone knew everyone, and the pub was the heart of the community. And just like the Lucky Prawn, the Narrandera Hotel had its classic Chinese restaurant, complete with the same red carpet and lanterns that I now saw before me. Growing up, we spent every second Christmas in that pub in Narrandera with the Dawson family.

As we over-ordered and ate our way through the honey chicken, sweet and sour pork, beef and black bean and the ubiquitous prawn crackers, I reminisced about countless meals spent in that restaurant, surrounded by family and friends. The food, perhaps not strictly authentic, was always comforting and familiar, a reminder of simpler times.

But it wasn't until I excused myself to visit the bathroom that I had a moment of pure nostalgia. As I pushed open the door, the unmistakable voices of Bill Lawry and Richie Benaud, the legendary Australian cricket commentators, greeted me. It was an old recording, of course — both are long since retired, with Benaud passing away in 2015 — but their voices instantly transported me back to the summers of my youth.

At that moment, I was no longer a middle-aged man in a Sydney brewery; I was a young boy again, sprawled in front of the television, watching the cricket with rapt attention. Lawry and Benaud's voices (along with others on the team) were the soundtrack of those lazy summer days, their commentary as much a part of the game as the crack of a ball on a bat.

As I stood there, memories washing over me, I was reminded of the immense power of nostalgia. The sights, sounds and tastes of our youth imprint on our psyche, shaping our experiences and understanding of the world. In that brewery, with its loving tribute to a bygone era, I reflected on how our past continues to influence our present, and how the language and voices we hear can transport us back in time.

**The sights, sounds and tastes of our youth imprint on our psyche, shaping our experiences and understanding of the world.**

Growing up, my brother and I had an unusual advantage — our parents owned an indoor cricket centre in Western Sydney. If you're unfamiliar, an indoor cricket centre is an enclosed facility with artificial pitches and protective nets, perfect for year-round batting practice. While other kids relied on their dads to bowl a few dozen balls in the nets on a hot midweek summer night, we had unlimited access to the centre's bowling machine — which could fire 500 balls at us in a single afternoon at speeds up to 160 kilometres per hour. At 12, we faced deliveries that would align with seasoned professionals.

Did the experience of facing blazing speeds on a bowling machine make us *naturally* gifted cricketers? I don't believe so. While my brother and I showed dedication by choosing to test ourselves against those extreme speeds, the unique environment we were immersed in is what primarily shaped our development and the skills we built from a young age. The indoor cricket facility, and specifically that menacing piece of bowling equipment, created an opportunity for accelerated growth that most aspiring players could not access. We constantly faced challenges that forced us to elevate our skills rapidly or be relentlessly exposed.

## INSIGHTS

This firsthand experience taught me a formative lesson about human potential that would echo through all my future endeavours — our surroundings and the opportunities available to us exert far more influence over our abilities than any innate, predetermined talent.

*(continued)*

Too often, incredible feats or creative breakthroughs are lazily attributed to someone's intrinsic gifts or inherent genius. But dig deeper and you'll usually find an environmental factor that acted as the real catalyst—the artistic prodigy raised with paints and canvases ever-present. The business visionary who was exposed to their parents' spirited dinner conversations about entrepreneurship. The musical virtuoso who heard complicated rhythms bouncing off the walls of their home.

We are incredibly malleable beings, especially from childhood. The inputs, resources, mentors, role models and learning environments profoundly shape our neural pathways. Talent has little to do with it. Ability is derived from sustained practice, quality coaching and being immersed in the right ecosystems.

My time subjected to that bowling machine's hostility provided an ideal microcosm. I may not have been born with preternatural hand-eye coordination, but that didn't matter because the environment quickly inculcated those skills out of necessity. By surrounding myself with high-performance equipment and tools and tough challenges from a young age, my capabilities grew to meet them. The environment was the decisive factor, not any innate gifts.

The implications here are far-reaching—and not limited to childhood. Your potential is not fixed but is instead responsive to the landscapes you situate yourself within. Transformative growth emerges by thoughtfully cultivating the personal, professional or creative ecosystems that will demand more of you. Your abilities expand when you purposefully engage in the right surroundings and opportunities. Environment, far more than talent alone, shapes who you ultimately become.

Some days, pushing our limits, my brother and I would dare crank the bowling machine to its highest setting—a terrifying 160 kilometres per hour, at that time faster than any professional bowler. I'm still amazed we didn't suffer serious injury testing those limits from the age of 12. But we didn't merely survive; we grew stronger, our reflexes sharpening from absorbing each punishing impact.

By age 16, we were easily turning away 150 kilometre-per-hour thunderbolts. So, when we progressed to higher-level competition, blistering pace was not the challenge. No, our biggest test was maintaining composure and discipline against relentless consistency from the bowlers. Our challenge was the same as anyone else:

maintaining discipline and commitment, patience and perseverance. It was an early lesson in the unwavering focus and determination required to lead and succeed.

I quickly learned that determining success requires more than just access. Sometimes, it's the most minor interactions that leave the most profound imprint. I remember being a young cricketer, progressing from the indoor cricket centre to nets training at Penrith, with dreams of playing cricket for Australia. My time training under John Benaud, a selector for the Australian test team and brother of the iconic Richie Benaud, was like a dream — until it wasn't. On Tuesdays and Thursdays, we'd each get 15 minutes to bat; a precious half-hour a week to hone our skills before the weekend's match. It was a chance to learn and to soak up wisdom from experienced coaches and senior players.

But those 15 minutes were often punctuated by shouts from the sidelines — from senior players, coaches and, in particular, my coach. John Benaud was an imposing figure, uncompromising in his traditional views on how the game should be played. If you dared loft one over the side netting, his bellow would slice through the air: 'Keep it in the bloody nets! We're not going on a bush walk to retrieve it, son.'

At 15 and 16 years old as I was, Benaud's snarls cut deep. Out there as a kid, boldly digging in against first-grade quicks — grown men with families, putting severe heat on it. Years of practice might coalesce for a split-second into a perfect shot, piercing the air over the netting. A textbook cricket stroke for the ages!

Not for Benaud! 'Rein it in, son!' he'd roar from the sidelines, almost disgusted at any hint of youthful ambition. He'd act like clearing the ropes was a crime, rather than a craft to be honed. As if blooding my lip against grown men wasn't dauntless enough without adding fury to their thunderbolts. Today, finding the car park from a cricket bat earns roars. But back then, any stroke revealing the audacity to aspire drew sneers and slapped wrists — the unmistakable message: pull your inflating head in, kid.

This type of reaction laid the foundation for the rest of my life, watching grown men, senior players and coaches poking holes, ribbing and jesting. Some people with good intentions can also do a lot of harm. I saw them, those coaches. I still do.

The cricket I saw prioritised conformity over the nurturing of individual skill and creativity. It morphed young men to be the same, to think like the coach or the senior players who hadn't lived up to their potential. They would offer advice as if their careers were blooming — kind, but often the wrong advice. The coaching usually took the form of systematic deflation, a series of mocking rebukes that chipped away at the confidence of young players. At an age when the mind is still malleable and prone to insecurity, having your aspirations briefly validated only to see them swiftly dismissed can be profoundly damaging. It plants seeds of doubt precisely where dreams should take root and flourish.

Such environments inadvertently impart a certain cruel wisdom. If you dare to dream beyond the confines of your current abilities, you'll find yourself perpetually chasing those ambitions alone in the wilderness. But this is antithetical to what the human spirit craves. We thrive on encouragement and mentors who empathise with our struggles and see life through our eyes. An authentic coach is defined not by their title but by their impact on those they guide. The focus should be on how they make you feel after an interaction, and the direction and clarity they provide. We need voices that urge us to keep swinging and pushing the boundaries of what we think we're capable of finding, now and then, another 1 per cent. In the truest sense, a coach is a catalyst for personal growth.

I found myself yearning for knowledgeable people who were eager to share their knowledge and who would patiently field the myriad questions that bubbled up in my curious mind. That desire for continuous learning and growth has stayed with me, becoming a lifelong fascination with the art of coaching and the science of high performance that verges on obsession.

## INSIGHTS

We often seek guidance, inspiration and motivation from external sources. Whether it's a coach shouting from the sidelines, a mentor offering wisdom or a creative workshop sparking new ideas, these experiences can profoundly shape our internal growth.

Most human development hinges on the presence of a guiding force—a foundation from which we can launch. These external influences become the building blocks of our future selves. They weave into the fabric of our being, shaping our habits, standards and aspirations. It's a gradual process, taking a lifetime to evolve.

I know now that most of our coaching is on our own. You are continually coaching yourself and cultivating internal disciplines. But sometimes, you may find yourself adrift, isolated from the guidance and leadership you crave.

As we age, all motivation becomes self-motivation. The key is recognising and harnessing the external forces that can catalyse your growth.

My final cricket trip was to Melbourne with the New South Wales under-19 team. The next step would be to play alongside grown men (no more juniors, which felt to me like no more fun), playing alongside men who had spent years in the system—a lot of unfulfilled dreams competing against each other. This was a turning point for me, and I felt a need for more inspiration. The world, I realised, was vast and full of possibilities. Spending my Saturdays and Sundays on a cricket pitch in an environment that didn't nurture my passion seemed a waste. I wanted something else. As I grew as a player and a person, I realised I needed to seek an environment that aligned with my values and aspirations. I needed to find a tribe that would stoke my ambition, not dampen it, and challenge me to push beyond my limits while providing the support and encouragement necessary. This realisation would shape my entire approach to life and learning.

I traded the cricket pitch for the ski slopes and the batting gloves for a snowboard. As one chapter drew to a close, that decision would alter the course of my life. Stepping away from the cricket pitch created a whole world of new possibilities. I set off for Canada, where I immersed myself in a new culture, environment and way of thinking.

Action sports and fashion branding gave me a creative outlet that I had been craving. It was a realm where innovation was celebrated and pushing boundaries was encouraged and expected. I threw myself into this new world with the same passion and determination I had once applied to cricket. Still, as I describe in chapter 1, I was driven not by external expectations but by an intrinsic desire to create, innovate and make my mark.

Being young is simply the beginning of a much larger adventure. The lessons I learned in sports—the importance of the environment, the power of perseverance and the necessity of challenging the status quo—would become the foundation for my future endeavours. But it was only over time, as I navigated the difficulties of business and life,

> **We need the courage to recognise that standing still is often more dangerous than change itself.**

that I fully grasped the significance of these experiences, and the lessons that they taught. One such lesson is the critical importance of empathy — the ability to understand and share the feelings of others. Success often hinges on our ability to put ourselves in someone else's shoes and see the world through their eyes.

But empathy alone is not enough. We need the courage to recognise that standing still is often more dangerous than change itself.

And so, we circle back to 2015, this time the morning of my 40th birthday. I couldn't help but reflect on the journey that had brought me to that point. Sitting in my garden that morning, my family still sleeping, I realised that the lessons of my youth had never left me. They evolved, shaping my approach to creativity, leadership and life. In that moment of clarity, as the music of Maroon 5 drifted through the air, I understood my story was still being written, that the challenges and triumphs of my cricketing days had been preparation for something greater — a life spent creating.

Here is what I wrote down that morning:

*It's early, 6 am, and the family are asleep. Today is my 40th birthday. I sneak out to check the surf, and my son has left Maroon 5 on Spotify. The track 'Sunday Morning' is a great wake-up track. The lyrics are so perfect.*

*Later, Nicola had cooked bacon. The kids had all made me a piece of wall-hanging art.*

*My breakfast marked my embrace of a new chapter. We sat in the garden, bacon and eggs, juice, coffee, three kids, one dog and my lovely partner ... this is perfect.*

*Short-lived perfection; as the routine 'let's get to school' tradition begins, kids, 'Get your shoes on; no, I haven't seen your school uniform; its sports day; what are you wearing, Kai? Why are you painting, Miff? Wait for your brother, no Pip and I can't come to school with you today ...'*

*Remember those lyrics from 'Sunday Morning,' their talk of still being together at the end.*

*Being alive for 40 years has taught me two things: how to lean in at the right time, and how to step aside when it feels right.*

*Such decisive life stepping and learning comes from a combination of perspectives, experiences and pressures. I have been an adult for 22 years; my businesses, the ones that worked and those that didn't, my relationships, the good ones, the bad, and the unwavering support from my wife, my friends and my family all help to shape me. For two decades, I have worked on building a home in a place we love, for the people I love, and with all the turbulence and emotion of the trials that occur in such a span of time, I feel content. I have failed and succeeded frequently. I have chosen adventure with all its challenges and twists, and it has landed me here.*

*Forty years brings about a particular awareness and efficiency in being oneself.*

*I have always subconsciously known that time, hourly, weekly and yearly, is a very fucking precious commodity. The time I am not prepared to waste.*

*So I lean in...*

*To the lessons. I have learnt the confidence that I am brave enough. Brave enough to lean in, brave enough to step aside.*

*So I lean in...*

*To ageing. I see it in my eyes, feel it in my knees and hold it in my hands daily. I want to age right, with a glass of red on a Friday night and the odd burger with fries. But as I age, so do my three kids, so I need to stay young enough to understand them but wise enough to let them age too, still healthy enough to stand beside them as we ride.*

*So I lean in...*

*To losing. I am okay with losing, not being elected, and being overlooked or ignored. I move on fast. If I were selected for everything, I would be playing life too safely; I don't want to play it safe. So I pursue opportunities, regardless of the result. I hope my kids do too.*

*So I lean in...*

*To art (some people call this work). I chose projects, clients and tasks that I believed in. That makes a difference. This is the time of my life when every minute contributed is valuable to me and someone else.*

*So I lean in...*

*To being healthy. I surf, ski, ride, walk and skate. By staying healthy, I stay young in mind. The ocean and the mountains are the world's best playgrounds. They cost nothing and give everything in return. I respect the mountains and the ocean and will continue my relationships with nature. I give my time freely as a ski patroller and a surf lifeguard, and I take back memorable moments. I know my kids do, too.*

*So I lean in…*

*To taking risks. I'm not playing it safe. Adventure comes first. It drives me.*

*So I lean in…*

*To accountability. I don't need to be asked to help. I can see it when someone needs someone. I know when I am wrong. If I need help, I will ask. If I am unsure, you will know. Chances are, I won't be; I will make a choice. Right or wrong. Hopefully right.*

*So I lean in…*

*To saying no as often as I say yes. In the future, unrealistic expectations will be met with a no.*

*And I step aside…*

*From changing what I have committed to. Nothing in the future is as important as the time I have already committed to now. I won't change a date for you if I have committed it to someone else. Ever.*

*I step aside…*

*From committees. I don't join committees.*

*I step aside…*

*From takers and time wasters.*

*I step aside…*

*From being a follower. I don't follow you. I join, partner and learn, but I don't follow.*

*So I lean in…*

*To the stories I tell myself about the things happening in my life — nothing but the truth in black and white. I will ask for help. I will not sit in silence wondering.*

*I appreciate the things in my life that offer the simplest pleasures: my friends and family. Everyone I love is healthy and alive; that will change in the future but, for now, I have battled enough setbacks and demons to know that when it shifts, I will find my way through. My mum has taught me that.*

*Until then, I will lean in when it counts, step aside when it doesn't, and make my life choices as an individual, a dad, a husband, a son, a business owner, a volunteer and a friend. Because at 40, they are the things that shape me.*

*That may be all I need.*

My mum, who I write about a lot in this book, passed away from cancer in 2018. She was a guiding force in my life, and I've included stories about her in later chapters that I know you'll love. As my family grows and evolves with my kids, Miff, Kai and Pip, and my nieces and nephews, Jack, Emily, Meghan, Cooper, Minnie and Xavier, I return to the lessons she taught me yearly. Her wisdom serves as a touchstone, reminding me of the values that have shaped my journey. Yet, among all the reflections, the hardest lesson has always been being honest with myself about the stories I tell — my life, my work and the things I avoid. It's a challenge I still wrestle with, but I know that embracing honesty is crucial for personal growth.

This is where creativity and you intersect. Creativity is simply the human act of doing something that might not work. It's problem-solving in its purest form. If you're sure something will work, that's not creativity — that's management. It took me years to learn that fear is the natural enemy of creativity. We're all born creative but, as we grow, we also grow afraid of judgement and failure. Too many voices tell us we can't, whether in the schoolyard, at cricket training or even at home. But here's what I've learned: creativity is the antidote to fear. The fear starts to fade when you act on your ideas and create. Action persuades fear to back off; over time, it shrinks or moves on.

You know that good idea you've had — lingering in the background for as long as you can remember? The hard part has never been having good ideas. The hard part is choosing and acting. It's about having the courage to pick one idea and put in the effort to bring it to life. That takes guts, but it's the only way forward. Saying 'I don't have any good ideas' is a cop-out. The challenge isn't about finding ideas but executing the ones you already have. The world doesn't need more devil's advocates; it needs more people willing to be brave enough to act.

# INSIGHTS

Your creativity isn't just shaped by what's within you; it's also deeply influenced by the spaces you inhabit and the company you keep. The right environment can ignite fresh ideas, while the wrong one might limit your potential. Finding your creativity is not solely about your skills or how hard you work; it's also about finding those physical and emotional spaces where creativity can flourish.

Take a moment to consider your surroundings: are they lifting you up or holding you back? You have the power to shape an environment that inspires growth and sparks creativity.

Don't just settle for the status quo—build a space that brings out the best in you.

As Brené Brown said, 'You can choose courage, or you can choose comfort. You cannot choose both'.

# CHAPTER 3
# **BLOWING IN THE WIND**

Understanding everything is connected
and interwoven

The morning air was biting; a relentless cold seemed to seep into my bones as I lay in a small, spartan unit in Creekside, Whistler, in Canada. It was 1997, I was 22, and my best mate Webby and I had arrived for the season early, full of anticipation for the winter ahead, hoping to be greeted by fresh, powdery snow. But the reality was we were complete novices, relying on a combination of word-of-mouth, newspapers and travel agents to guide our journey.

As I reflect on that time now, it's clear to me that some of the best decisions in life come not from well-laid plans but from a willingness to embrace the unconventional. We weren't following a script; we were simply following our instincts. Creativity often works this way — sometimes, the journey is less about what you know and more about what you're willing to explore. It's about daring to step off the well-trodden path, even if it means stepping into uncertainty.

Our little place in Creekside was a far cry from luxury — no TV, no phone, just the essentials. But it was the foundation for the adventure we had been dreaming of for so long. Looking back, our early arrival in November, before Whistler even opened, was a testament to our naivety and the lack of reliable information. With no internet to guide us, we were at the mercy of pretty clueless travel agents and a general lack of knowledge about Whistler's seasonal rhythms.

A year earlier, I had decided to leave cricket. The endless loop of technique dissections, strategy debates and post-game analyses had worn thin. For me, the decision to leave cricket in the rear-view was as natural as breathing. It was time to break the cycle, to shatter the mould that had shaped my life for so long.

And so, with Webby as my co-pilot, we charted a course for Canada. We hustled and scraped, turning over every couch cushion and raiding every piggy bank. I even parted ways with the family car, a hand-me-down from my mum. But the real ace up my sleeve was my cricket gear. Growing up, I'd had the privilege of being sponsored by Gunn & Moore, a cricket equipment and apparel company. They must have seen a spark of potential in me because they kept me flush with a never-ending supply of pristine, plastic-wrapped bats. Once I left the sport, I knew those bats were now my golden ticket to North America. I sold them off, piece by piece, and the proceeds covered my airfare and then some.

Word got out, and suddenly friends were coming out of the woodwork, eager to snag even my pads and gloves for $5 a pop. Some were fresh off the shelf, never touched by a ball. But I wasn't about to get sentimental. Every dollar, every cent, represented another day on the slopes, another chance to immerse myself in something new.

Now we were finally in Canada, and Webby and I were young, brave and determined. The mountain may have been closed, with opening day still ten days away, but we had other plans. We refused to let the minor inconvenience of a closed resort — and closed chair lifts — dampen our spirits. With a sense of purpose and a thirst for adventure, we packed our backpacks and set out to conquer the Whistler Peak to Creek ski run on our terms. It's a monster of a run, stretching 11 kilometres with a descent that drops 1529 metres. But first we had to get there.

The cold nipped at our faces as we hiked through the silent, snow-covered landscape. Every breath was a visible puff of condensation, a reminder of the harsh conditions we were braving. We were armed with just our new boards, ready to tackle a trail we'd only dreamed of, far from the familiar flatness of Benson's Lane back in Richmond, Sydney, where our biggest worry was dodging flies and getting through the 40-degree arvos. But with each step, we felt a growing sense of exhilaration and freedom, a rush of adrenaline that comes from forging your path. We were going to find fresh tracks, consequences be damned. It was a moment of unadulterated rebellion against the constraints of the ordinary. We were two young men on a mission, fuelled by a burning desire to experience something raw and honest that would etch itself into our memories for a lifetime.

As we stepped through the snow, each crunch revealed the mountain's rugged bones — rocks and pebbles hidden under the fresh powder from the previous day's heavy snowfall. It was raw, untouched and unforgiving. We trudged on, feeling the mountain push back against our every step; the distance from the car park to the ski lift at Perisher never felt this long.

A couple of hours in, we collapsed onto a rock, catching our breath. We had clawed our way up only 400 metres of the 1529 drop. Below, the village seemed smaller, a quiet witness to our audacity. We laughed, not because our goal was absurd but because we had underestimated the challenge. Yet, there was something pure about being here, in the thick of nature.

By midday, with the sun glaring down, it hit us — we were around 625 metres up, surrounded by a silent white expanse. 'Not quite the summit, eh?' Webby's voice cut through the cold.

'Far from it', I answered, staring at the seemingly endless path ahead.

Our journey had morphed from a physical challenge to something more profound. We became acutely aware of the minor details — the crunch underfoot, the distant call of a raven and the shifting winds that hinted at a storm brewing. With our boards now feeling heavier with respect rather than just weight, Webby stood up, dusting off the snow. 'Let's push a bit further, see the next marker, then call it', he proposed, already looking up the trail. 'Creek to creek today, peak another day', he murmured.

Agreeing, we strapped on our packs. We took about 20 more steps, stopped, looked at each other and erupted into laughter! Who were we kidding? In an almost unified knowing glance, we agreed it was time to head down!

What took three hours to ascend took mere minutes to descend. We zipped down the mountain, the fresh, untouched snow under our boards making us feel like we were flying — until we weren't. Our naïve belief that all snow was the same was quickly corrected; the pristine fresh snow without a base meant our boards found every hidden rock and patch of gravel beneath. In my head, I had pictured us gliding effortlessly like in those Warren Miller ski and snowboarding films, but reality had other plans. Every hidden obstacle along the slope made its presence known.

Yet, we laughed through it all, whooping and cheering, catching each other's eyes and bursting into laughter again. Our descent was a chaotic ballet of joy and jarring jolts. When we reached the bottom, our new snowboards were etched with battle scars — gouges and scratches that mapped out our reckless journey down.

But something profound shifted in me that day. At 22, hurtling down that mountain, I tasted true freedom. It was a freedom not just from the physical constraints of urban life but also from the expectations that had quietly shaped my path. The mountain was indifferent to my history or future, offering only its slopes' raw, immediate challenge. The people I met in Whistler, adventurers from around the globe, were all drawn by similar desires. Their positivity and relentless pursuit of new challenges and uncharted paths struck a deep chord within me.

This trip was more than just a holiday; it was a foundational experience, shaping my views on what it meant to live. At 22, these mountains offered me a glimpse of a different existence rooted in adventure and discovery. It was an insight that wouldn't leave me. Two decades later, at 41, the echo of that freedom would pull me away from my own company, pushing me to redefine my life to rediscover myself.

The mountains, it turned out, were not just a place to visit—they were a call to something greater, something enduringly wild within me.

◊◊◊

People always ask me why I chose snow. What fascinated me? It's a fair question, especially for someone who spent their entire childhood trying to make a name for himself in cricket. I had played for NSW, honed my skills in elite academies and even had a stint as an overseas pro in the United Kingdom. But the decision to pivot to snow was as clear as a crisp winter morning for me. The reasons all boiled down to my dad, good music and the year 1985.

Mum and Dad were always determined parents, wanting to give us the best upbringing and experiences they could. But, like me, my mum and dad were self-starters, entrepreneurs forging their path. They loved adventures and taking us to new places, and were always determined to give us a memorable experience despite their tight budget. In 1985, they decided it was time for our first family trip to the snow. With a tent in tow and excitement bubbling, we piled into the car and headed for Jindabyne, a winter tourist town in the NSW mountains.

Before hitting the road, Mum had to head to the shops to grab supplies and other bits and pieces. I used to love going into the local music store and thumbing through the tapes and vinyl. I was obsessed with the idea of portable music. My Walkman went with me everywhere, and I still have my first one in storage. So, as Mum shopped, I decided to check out what was on offer.

Before I walked into the music store in Penrith Plaza, Mum handed me a $10 note and told me to grab something for the road trip, a soundtrack to remember it by. This was my first memory of independently purchasing anything; it is vivid. I was immediately drawn to INXS's *Listen Like Thieves*, the just-released album that everyone was talking about. Owning that tape was a step towards being cool like the older kids I admired. At $7.99, marked down to $5.99, my mind raced. (Firstly, why was it 1 cent short of $6 and, secondly, holy heck, maybe I could buy two tapes?) But the maths was against me; two tapes would cost $12, a small fortune!

Undeterred, I kept browsing! Then I spotted *1985 Comes Alive*, a perfect compilation album with neon writing jumping off the cover — also boasting 'original artists' and 'original hits'. The album cover is as crisp in my mind today as it was then. The album itself offered all kinds of songs and artists in one: 'The Wild Boys' by Duran Duran, 'Sexcrime (Nineteen Eighty-Four)' by Eurythmics, 'Caribbean Queen (No More Love on the Run)' by Billy Ocean, 'Cruel Summer' from Bananarama, 'NeverEnding Story' by Limahl and 'The Unforgettable Fire' by U2, just to name a few. (U2 would later go on to become the soundtrack to my adolescence.) At $9, it marked down to $5, still bringing my total to $1 more than I had.

As I walked the aisles of the store, holding my choices, I was also holding another album, almost without realising it — Dire Straits' *Brothers in Arms*. I wasn't sure about it. I remember the cover didn't grab me like the one for *Listen Like Thieves* did, but something about it meant I couldn't put it down. Maybe the classic 'Money for Nothing' song, which still takes me back to that store when I hear it.

I waited by the cash register for Mum to arrive. When she turned up, I handed her *Listen Like Thieves* and *1985 Comes Alive*. She smiled and said I was short.

'Please, Mum', I begged; it was only $1. Sure enough, without hesitation, Mum coughed up the extra $1.

'What about that one?' she asked, pointing to *Brothers in Arms*. 'Are you buying that?' I said we couldn't afford it, and put it to the side. As we jumped into the Ford Telstar to head home, however, Mum put on a tape she had purchased when I wasn't looking: *Brothers in Arms* from Dire Straits. She'd decided to get it for me anyway. That was Mum: generous and always full of surprises.

The same afternoon, we drove to Jindabyne. Dad's silver Ford Telstar became a jukebox. Dad belted out Elvis classics, and Mum played her favourite Dolly Parton and Kenny Rogers tapes, but it was INXS on my Walkman for me. I played *Listen Like Thieves* on repeat, and shouted along to the lyrics. It made me feel strong, like I was part of something bigger. Dad would glare back as I sang, drowning out Kenny Rogers or Gene Pitney in the front.

As the mountains rolled by, our first snowy adventures lay ahead, and I felt a newfound sense of freedom and possibility. I sang loudly and proudly, heading into nature and the mountains. But, in reality, I was heading into a doorway that would usher in a new phase of my life. A good song is like a time machine; that may be why we hold them so tightly. Songs are more than sounds — they invite the world to open up around us to explore past adventures.

Even now, in meetings, I find myself doodling '85', '1985' and even 'Choose Life' (for me, the slogan of the 1980s, made famous by Wham's t-shirts in the 'Wake Me Up Before You Go-Go' film clip). A subconscious tribute to a year that shaped me in ways I'm still discovering.

◊◊◊

That morning, the chill in Jindabyne, even in October, was unlike anything I'd ever experienced. Temperatures on the mountain can drop quickly at any time of the year, sometimes to a bone-numbing –10 degrees. It was a stark contrast to the temperatures we were used to in Penrith, and we were under-prepared, equipped with just jeans and jumpers, sleeping in a tent. I remember it being a long night out there, braving the cold, but my excitement for skiing was overpowering any discomfort. The anticipation of gliding down the slopes as soon as it was light was enough to keep me warm. On the other hand, Mum made no secret of her disdain for the freezing temperatures. I am 100 per cent certain she only returned to the snowy mountains when my kids competed in snowboarding and ski competitions some 30 years later.

Our first day on the mountain was short, but in my mind, it lasted forever. A full-day ticket proved too steep for our modest budget, so we skied from 9 am to 12 pm. But in those few hours, I discovered a new world. Learning to stand on the snow and navigate my first turns was pure magic. I was that kid who couldn't bear to take off his skis, savouring every last second on the snow, walking through the car park with his skis on. I remember trying to sneak in an extra run through the car park. The ski hire company must have been thrilled with the returned ski condition.

Those early experiences sparked a love affair with the mountains that would define my life. The mountains would steal my cricket career and, later, my company. But not my dreams. They never stole those; instead, the mountains and nature found a way to feed them.

While my brother and mum were content to stay home after that first visit, Dad and I embarked on weekend pilgrimages to Jindabyne in the coming years. Rising at an ungodly 3 am, we'd embark on the long, five-hour drive, arriving just in time for a full day on the slopes. Exhausted but elated, we'd then return home, only to do it again the following weekend. This became a ritual we would continue for almost a decade. My dad was my original snow partner. He was the first to show me the mountains and understand how they made me feel. So, he found the time to keep showing me the mountains.

Those countless hours spent in the car with Dad were as valuable as the time on the mountain. The stories we shared, the laughter, the comfortable silences — it was during those drives that I truly got to know my father. He opened up in ways he never had before, sharing tales that will forever remain between us. I know deep down my dad's love of sport, cricket and rugby league. He wanted me to be a pro cricketer but took me, anyway. For Dad, my happiness was his genuine desire. Through those trips, I developed a deep respect and admiration for him that would only grow with time. Until I turned 20, we would, together, just the two of us, find our way to the mountains and, in turn, the mountains would help us find a way to each other. Maybe it was his way of connecting with me. It worked.

I often say nature makes me feel alive, but it is deeper than that. The people and places that touch us give us hope, clarity and belief. My dad was a dreamer, and I have never doubted that his biggest dream was seeing his boys content.

My dad and his sacrifices to indulge my passion forged our connection. I doubt he loved the snow and skiing as much as I did, but he never hesitated to pack up the car and drive me to the mountain, week after week, year after year. That selfless dedication and unwavering support meant much more than any team talk on a community cricket pitch in Bankstown on a hot summer day.

# INSIGHTS

I've long thought the age-old debate of 'nature versus nurture' is misguided. To me, nature *is* nurture. The mountains, with their raw and rugged splendour, offer healing that can't be synthesised. They are cathedrals where we go to mend, grow and find peace away from the constructs of modern society.

In today's world, the assault of screen time can detach us from the essential human experience. I see the mountains as an antidote to our digital dependencies. In this physical and mental sanctuary, the only notifications are the calls of distant wildlife or the rustle of leaves. The ocean, too, serves as my meditation space—vast, rhythmic and perpetually present. In these expanses, we all can find the importance of solitude, where the mind can wander freely without the constraints of artificial urgency.

Creativity is born from discovery. We all enter this world as creators, curious and full of potential. Over time, societal norms can dilute this innate creativity, steering us toward what scales and pays. We're told that art, sports and spontaneity are luxuries few can afford; they don't often scale. Seth Godin has a different take on art; he defines art as having nothing to do with the painting. It is all about making *something*—a business, a product, a life, a choice! Art is a profoundly human endeavour—a gift that dares to disrupt, crafted to transform its audience and forge new connections. It embodies five elusive qualities: humanity, generosity, risk, transformation and connectivity.

Life offers us three choices:

1. Strive for perfection or create art.
2. Count returns or create art.
3. Maintain the existing or create art.

The greatest challenge is deciding to make art and embracing the demands it places on you. When I forgot how to make art at the age of 41, my art was to become a great dad, to take my kids and family on an adventure to rediscover what my art was.

Yet, the key isn't to follow passion blindly but to follow creativity—the simple act of being open to discovery. Creativity isn't about waiting for inspiration to strike; it's about engaging with the world, experimenting and allowing yourself to be led by curiosity rather than expectation. When you follow creativity, you're not tied to a single passion or rigid outcome. Instead, you're pursuing something fluid and evolving that grows with you.

This pursuit, honed through dedication—those famed 10000 hours (true or not) identified by Malcolm Gladwell in *Outliers*—eventually transforms into passion. Once nurtured, creativity shapes the work you do, how you approach problems, and how you explore opportunities. And with time, what may have started as uncertainty blossoms into a deep-seated passion for the process.

Every day becomes an adventure, every challenge an opportunity to craft your art. You learn to see obstacles not as roadblocks but as the moments when creativity thrives the most. The best solutions, the most profound ideas, often come from navigating the unconventional, from finding new ways when the old ones no longer serve you. This is the essence of creativity: staying open to what might be and, in that openness, finding your path forward.

The contrast between a natural high and a synthetic one couldn't be starker. No chemical concoction can replicate the exhilaration of conquering a peak or riding the first wave at dawn. Nature offers a pure and refreshing high—it saves, inspires and answers the unspoken questions.

I know and have heard parents and colleagues stick all sorts of labels on me for uprooting my life at 41 and immersing my children in mountainous terrains where snow is both playground and teacher—calling me an ambitious father, uncompromising, fierce, strict, mad and crazy. Yes, I am all those things—demanding, pushy and ambitious. But, above all, I am a father committed to teaching resilience, creativity and the pure joy of a life on the edge of possibility.

With my family, our world became smaller as we travelled together, learning from each other and evolving. In the mountains, we defined what was possible, each slope a lesson, each fall a story.

To be creative is to be empathetic, to understand the ebb and flow of human emotion deeply, and to translate that into something tangible. One of my heroes, the late

> **To be creative is to be empathetic, to understand the ebb and flow of human emotion deeply, and to translate that into something tangible.**

Sir Ken Robinson, advocated creativity. His work called for creative change in educational systems and personal development. His belief that 'creativity is as important in education as literacy' was so important to me. Robinson famously posited that schools kill creativity, urging us to foster an environment where children — and indeed all individuals — can retain and nurture their innate creative capacities. He argued, 'We stigmatise mistakes in school, mistakes are the worst thing you can make. We are educating our kids out of their creative capacities.'

Robinson's insights helped reshape my approach to work and design. They reminded me of the value of staying curious and open, qualities that would guide my later career in humanity-centred design. As a designer, I've had the privilege of reimagining and reshaping brands, businesses, software and environments. I've designed everything from buildings to eyewear, from socks to software, and advised significant global companies such as Australia Post, BHP, Gulf Oil and Westpac on the transformative power of design. (Side note, as a B Corp, we don't work with fossil fuel companies anymore.)

In 2012, amid the troubled rollout of Australia Post's first digital mailbox, when seething press coverage and financial losses mounted, my company was the one they turned to for a way forward. The challenge was immense, requiring Australia Post to shift from traditional to digital mail — a transformation affecting every organisational facet. Sitting in those boardroom sessions, I was overwhelmed, questioning my place at the table. Yet, my willingness to embrace risk and the possibility of failure was why I was there.

Creativity isn't just about producing art or innovative designs; it's a broader capability essential to solving complex problems and leading meaningful change. The path less trodden is not only valid but also vital. Creativity is about finding your way, and stepping off the well-walked path to discover routes unimagined by others. Just keep moving forward. The answers will find you.

Living creatively means living a life of discovery and curiosity, being willing to embrace the unknown. By adopting these principles, you not only enhance your life but also have the potential to change the world around you. This is the power of design and creative thinking. Let's carry this understanding forward, using it to fuel every step of our journey.

As Sir Ken Robinson said, 'If you're not prepared to be wrong, you'll never come up with anything original.'

# INSIGHTS

The best creative work often comes when you let go of what's familiar and follow your instincts. It's not about doing more—it's about doing less and simplifying so the real idea can come forward. Sometimes, stepping away from routine or taking a different route leads to unexpected breakthroughs.

Creativity isn't found in the apparent answers; it's discovered when you dare to explore new directions, even if they go against the grain. Whether you're facing a new project, a career choice or a personal move, trust your gut, clear away the clutter and take a bold step into the unknown. The best ideas often lie just off the beaten path.

## PART II

# JUNCTIONS: PURPOSE

### Where crossroads appear, and purpose shapes the direction of your creative journey

I've faced many forks on the road, and each one taught me that purpose is the foundation of creative confidence. It's not just what you create that's important, but also *why* you make it. Purpose aligns your efforts with something deeper and more meaningful, guiding you through the rough patches. When you know your 'why', the 'what' becomes clearer, and your confidence in your creative choices grows stronger.

# CHAPTER 4

# NORTH BY SOUTHWEST (AIRLINES)

Choosing your creative path at the intersection of opportunity and intention

In spring 1999, I boarded a Southwest Airlines flight from Vancouver to San Francisco. As we boarded, I couldn't help but notice the lively energy that seemed to permeate the cabin. The flight attendants stood out with their warm smiles and genuine enthusiasm, a refreshing change from the usually stoic and impersonal attitude I'd experienced on other airlines.

I had just spent the winter working at Grouse Mountain in Vancouver as a snowboard instructor. Nicola had flown back to London to see her family. I was travelling to San Francisco for a few days to catch up with our friend Sumo, who had once worked for Disney in Los Angeles but was now based in San Fran. Sumo had promised a fun few days before I headed over to London to see Nicola. We planned to catch a few shows, such as *Rent* (the musical) and the Goo Goo Dolls, and see the sights. I was a broke snowboarder living day-to-day, while Sumo was a high-flying marketing executive with connections. I was excited to catch up.

The flight took off smoothly, and I settled into the journey, eagerly anticipating our arrival in one of my favourite cities on earth. As we approached, however, an unexpected challenge arose. The fog that San Francisco is famous for had blanketed the city, obscuring the airport and making landing impossible.

The captain's voice crackled over the intercom, informing us we would need to circle above the airport until the fog cleared and it was safe to land. A wave of disappointment travelled through the passengers in the cabin as they listened to the captain's announcement, realising that their plans and schedules would be disrupted.

Restlessness and frustration settled over the passengers as the minutes ticked by and the plane circled. The confined space of the aircraft, coupled with the uncertainty of when we would land, created tension in the air.

During this time of uncertainty and unease, something remarkable happened. The Southwest Airlines flight attendants, famous for their humour and quick thinking, assembled in the aisles. With mischievous grins on their faces and a twinkle in their eyes, they burst into an impromptu singalong.

As the opening notes of 'I've Been Working on the Railroad' filled the cabin, the flight attendants all joined a lively rendition of the classic American folk song, encouraging the passengers to also sing along. At first, there was a moment of surprised silence as the unexpected musical interlude caught everyone off guard. But then, something magical happened. One by one, passengers joined in, their voices rising in unison to meet the flight attendants' melodious lead. From front to back, the entire plane became a chorus of joyful singing, the frustration and tension of just moments before melting away in the face of this spontaneous display of camaraderie.

I sat there, amazed at the transformation taking place around me. A sense of unity and shared experience had replaced the once-stifling atmosphere of the plane. Strangers silently enduring the delay were now bonding over this moment of musical connection.

As the song continued, laughter and smiles spread throughout the cabin. The flight attendants' faces were alive with joy, and they moved up and down the aisles, encouraging passengers to sing louder and join in the fun. It was a scene that defied the typical air travel expectations, and a moment of unadulterated human connection in the most unlikely places.

Amid the joyful chaos of the impromptu singalong, I was a 24 year old who considered himself way too cool to join in the folksy amusement. As much as the unexpected turn of events amazed me, I couldn't help but feel a sense of awkwardness wash over me. While the rest of the passengers enthusiastically belted out the lyrics, I sat there, nodding in encouragement and offering half-hearted smiles to those around me.

'Well done', I mouthed silently to the singing passengers, trying to show my support without actually joining in. Feeling out of place and self-conscious, I couldn't embrace the moment. Making eye contact with the flight attendants became an uncomfortable game of avoidance. They would catch my gaze, clap and smile, leaning in as if to say, 'It's your turn now!' But I quickly diverted my eyes, seeking solace in the view outside the aeroplane window.

The singing continued, tearing me between admiration for the flight attendants' ability to create such a joyful atmosphere and a growing desire to disappear into my seat. The window became my refuge, allowing me to temporarily escape the participatory pressure. I focused on the clouds and the distant horizon, hoping the singalong would soon end and spare me from any further awkwardness.

Little did I know that this discomfort would soon lead to a profound conversation that would change my perspective on the power of brands and the importance of human connection. For now, though, I remained the awkward 24 year old, silently observing the surrounding merriment. I was not quite ready to let go of my reservations and join in the chorus of unity that filled the Southwest Airlines cabin.

Thinking about this experience now, it reminds me of something fundamental about creativity—it's about more than just clever solutions or ideas. At its essence, creativity is about connection. It's about creating moments that resonate, no matter how small. I know now that the most meaningful creative work emerges when driven by a real desire to connect with others. Whether through a design, a story or even a simple act of kindness, creativity becomes most powerful when it aims to bring people closer, foster empathy and create shared experiences.

> **Creativity is about more than just clever solutions or ideas. At its essence, creativity is about connection.**

Travelling with Southwest Airlines for the first time altered my understanding of brands' power and the community's importance. Southwest Airlines stands out as a company that dares to be different, challenging the conventions of an industry that had grown stale and complacent.

# INSIGHTS

Founded in 1967 by the visionary Herb Kelleher, Southwest Airlines set out to revolutionise the world of air travel. They rejected the traditional high fares and frills airline model, instead embracing a low-cost, no-frills approach that prioritised efficiency, accessibility and customer service. They made a bold move in an industry that had long been dominated by legacy carriers who seemed more interested in protecting their turf than innovating for the benefit of their passengers.

At the heart of Southwest's strategy was a focus on short, direct flights and minimal turnaround times. By optimising their aircraft utilisation, they could offer more daily flights, making air travel more accessible to a broader range of customers. This approach helped keep costs down, and ensured that Southwest's planes spent more time in the air, generating revenue, than on the ground, gathering dust.

Southwest's decision to eschew assigned seating was one of its most striking departures from industry norms. Instead, they implemented an open seating policy, allowing passengers to choose their seats on a first-come, first-served basis. This innovative approach streamlined the boarding process, reducing the time planes spent idling at the gate and enabling Southwest to maintain its impressive turnaround times.

While other airlines battled for precious slots at crowded major hubs, Southwest strategically focused on secondary airports. By flying into these less congested airports, Southwest avoided the delays and inefficiencies plaguing its competitors while offering its passengers a more accessible travel experience.

Southwest's unconventional approach proved it was possible to offer low fares without compromising quality or customer service. They made air travel fun again, injecting a sense of joy and humanity into an industry that had grown increasingly impersonal and transactional.

However, the most remarkable aspect of Southwest's success was its deep commitment to its people. Herb Kelleher and his team recognised that happy, engaged employees were the key to creating an exceptional customer experience. They fostered a culture of empowerment, creativity and teamwork, encouraging employees to bring their whole selves to work and have fun.

This emphasis on culture and community was more than just a feel-good strategy; it was a fundamental driver of Southwest's success. By creating an environment where employees feel valued, respected and engaged, Southwest could attract and keep top talent while building a sense of loyalty and enthusiasm among their customers.

As I experienced firsthand on that flight, Southwest's unique approach to air travel was about more than just getting passengers from point A to point B. It was about creating a sense of connection and shared humanity, in an industry that had grown cold and impersonal. It was a reminder that businesses can shape their bottom lines *and* the lives and experiences of the people they serve.

As I stepped off the plane and onto the jet bridge, my mind was still processing the unexpected events that had transpired during the flight. The fog delay, the impromptu singalong — it had all been surreal. I was eager to put the experience behind me and finish my day, but fate had other plans.

Just as I was about to make my way towards the terminal, a flight attendant approached me. She had a warm, friendly demeanour, but there was a hint of curiosity in her eyes. 'Excuse me', she said, 'but are you Ben Rennie?'

It surprised me. How did she know my name? 'Yes, I am', I confirmed, hesitantly.

For a moment, a flicker of excitement coursed through me. Could this be about the delay? Were they going to offer me a complimentary flight for the inconvenience? It seemed too good to be true.

But the flight attendant's next question quickly dispelled any such notions. 'Mr Rennie', she said, her tone gentle but probing, 'I couldn't help but notice that you didn't join in the singing earlier. It seemed like you wanted to be anywhere but in that situation. Is everything alright?'

I felt a rush of heat on my cheeks — embarrassment mixed with a twinge of defensiveness. I hadn't meant to be rude, but the singing wasn't my scene. 'Oh, well', I stumbled, trying to find the right words. 'It's just that singing isn't my thing. That was not for me.'

The stewardess nodded, her expression understanding. She paused for a moment as if contemplating her following words. 'Well, Mr Rennie', she said finally, 'thank you for flying with us today. We may be a small airline, but I want you to know that our people take great pride in our business and culture.'

I nodded, unsure of where this conversation was going.

'Do you know why we don't wear uniforms on the flight?' she asked.

I shook my head, feeling awkward. I hadn't given it much thought.

'It's so we can keep our costs low,' she explained, her voice filled with conviction. 'We can provide more air travel access by stripping away unnecessary expenses, like fancy uniforms. Everyone deserves the opportunity to fly, regardless of their budget.'

I nodded again, understanding Southwest's unconventional approach. A deeper purpose was behind it.

The stewardess continued; her passion for her work was clear in every word. 'You see, Mr. Rennie, we're not just an airline at Southwest. We're a community. We believe that by connecting people, by making travel affordable and accessible, we can make a real difference in people's lives.'

She went on to share stories of families reunited and dreams fulfilled, all made possible by Southwest's commitment to its mission. As she spoke, I felt a shift within myself. My initial discomfort and embarrassment faded, replaced by a growing sense of admiration and respect.

Here was a company focused on not just the bottom line but also truly serving its customers and communities. It recognised the power of human connection and was willing to do things differently to foster it.

As we parted ways, the flight attendant's words stayed with me. 'I hope you'll give us another chance, Mr Rennie,' she said warmly. 'And next time, maybe you'll even join in the singing.'

I laughed, surprised that the idea didn't seem daunting anymore.

**A brand is more than just a logo or a slogan — it could be a force for good, a catalyst for positive change.**

That conversation, brief as it was, profoundly impacted me. It opened my eyes to the idea that a brand can be more than just a logo or a slogan — it could be a force for good, a catalyst for positive change.

As I look back on that walk through the terminal, I reflect on the power of authentic human connection and the role that brands can play in fostering it. This lesson would shape my career later in life, honing my understanding of business, leadership and the transformative potential of purpose-driven organisations.

Reflecting on that moment, I realise it was a turning point — not just in my professional journey, but also in my personal growth. It taught me to look beyond the surface to seek the more profound meaning and purpose behind the brands and companies I interacted with.

# INSIGHTS

When entering the established airline industry, Southwest recognised its constraints. Often perceived as obstacles or limitations, constraints are the secret weapon of innovation and growth. When wielded strategically, they propel your vision to new heights. Far from being roadblocks, constraints force you to distil your ideas to their very essence, stripping away the extraneous and leaving only what truly matters.

When faced with financial, temporal or resource-based constraints, the natural human response is to feel stifled and that options are limited. But these moments of apparent scarcity are precisely when the most creative solutions are born. Constraints demand that you think differently, approach problems from unconventional angles and explore avenues you might have overlooked.

In business, constraints are the catalysts that spark innovation. They can compel you to make strategic decisions and prioritise ruthlessly, focusing your efforts on what will yield the most significant impact. When resources are limited, you are forced to be resourceful. When time is short, you learn to be efficient. And when the odds seem stacked against you, you can dig deep and find reserves of creativity and resilience you never knew you possessed.

But the power of constraints extends beyond problem-solving. They are also the key to unlocking a more profound sense of purpose and humanity in your work. When forced to operate within certain boundaries, you must confront what truly matters, what you stand for and what you are willing to fight for. Constraints strip away the superficial and the superfluous, giving you a clearer sense of your core values and the impact you want to make in the world.

I love the power of crucible moments coming into play. Throughout your life and careers, you will encounter moments that can shape your trajectory, clarify your goals, and refine your creative visions. These moments might come as a chance encounter, a sudden insight or a challenging experience that

*(continued)*

forces you to question everything you thought you knew. Call them your crucible moment when you see them, where you feel a shift.

The key is recognising crucible moments when they arise and harnessing their transformative potential. When you find yourself stuck or uncertain, it's easy to feel paralysed by indecision or overwhelmed by the complexity of your challenges. But if you can train yourself to look for the signs and find inspiration in life's cracks and crevices, you open yourself up to a world of possibility.

Through my career and businesses, I have worked with some of the world's most iconic brands, from Ray-Ban and Oakley to Dolce & Gabbana, Patagonia, Chanel, Nike, Adidas, Westpac and Australia Post. These brands are more than just names or logos; they are also symbols of connection and influence, values and aspirations.

Through my work with these brands, I have had the incredible opportunity to meet and connect with people from all walks of life. From a night out in Milan with Valentino Rossi to a dinner party with Hugh Jackman to a lifelong friendship with Tim Ross, I have forged these connections through a shared passion for the brands that bring us together.

A brand's power to create community and spark meaningful relationships is remarkable. When we rally around a brand that speaks to our values and desires, we become part of something bigger than ourselves. We connect with others who share our passions and sense of purpose; in doing so, we open ourselves up to a world of adventure, creativity and growth.

The genuine gift of working with great brands is the opportunity to be part of something that matters, to make a real difference in people's lives, and to forge connections that last a lifetime. This lesson has stayed with me throughout my career, and I carry it with me in everything I do.

But the power of brands goes beyond just personal connections. The brands we associate with, the ones we wear on our sleeves and carry in our hearts, define us in ways we might not even realise. They reflect our values, aspirations and sense of self. When we align ourselves with a brand that connects with who we are and what we stand for, we make a statement about the person we want to be in the world.

This is why building and nurturing great brands is so critical. It's about not only selling products or services but also shaping the choices and behaviours of people across the globe. It's about creating something that inspires and uplifts, that brings people together and helps them find their place in the world.

Reflecting on my journey and lessons, I am struck by the incredible power of creativity and innovation to transform the world. Whether through the design of a great product, the creation of a compelling brand, or the forging of meaningful connections and relationships, our work as creative professionals has the power to shape the future in profound and lasting ways.

**Our work as creative professionals has the power to shape the future in profound and lasting ways.**

Seek the moments that define you, the experiences that shape your vision and sense of purpose. Above all, never stop learning, never stop growing and never stop pushing yourself to be the best version of yourself.

The world is waiting for you. The problems are waiting to be solved, and the opportunities are waiting to be seized. Make your mark. Create something beautiful and meaningful that makes a difference in people's lives. And know that with every step you take, every connection you forge and every problem you solve, you are part of something bigger than yourself—a global community of creatives and change makers shaping the future, one idea at a time.

## INSIGHTS

At its heart, creativity is all about connection. It's more than just solving problems; it's about creating moments that truly resonate with others. Creative confidence comes to life when it's fuelled by purpose and a sincere desire to connect—whether through words, design or a fresh idea.

The magic of creativity doesn't lie in trying to impress; it lies in expressing something genuine and meaningful. When you focus on the human experience, your work transcends simple functionality and becomes something that truly matters.

Think about your next creative move: how can it bring people closer, inspire empathy or create a shared experience? Don't just aim to be clever—aim to connect.

# CHAPTER 5

Finding the value in purpose and how it drives your creativity

In 2007, the streets of Milan buzzed with anticipation of the grand opening of the Gold restaurant, an opulent venue brought to life by the iconic duo Dolce & Gabbana. The event fused fashion with nightlife in a way only Stefano Gabbana and Domenico Dolce could envision, and it was a spectacle of glamour and exclusivity. I arrived on the red carpet alongside Samantha De Kauwe, a creative marketing leader at Luxottica Group, who would later influence major Australian brands such as Sass & Bide and Sportscraft and her family's venture, The Critical Slide Society. I reminded myself of a key lesson: creativity thrives in the unpredictable.

Stefano and Domenico greeted us at the door, at the end of the red carpet amid flashing cameras and noise and bustle from fans lining the streets, a surreal moment that marked the beginning of an unforgettable night. Inside, the restaurant glimmered with golden décor; the air was thick and had extraordinary promise. It wasn't long before I found myself face to face with footballer Cristiano Ronaldo and his partner. However, my acute sense of feeling out of place overshadowed the brief exchange. Despite his polite nod, I couldn't shake the feeling that he had more critical guests to attend to. Dressed in an Oxford suit and Windsor Smith shoes, I felt distinctly like a boy from Penrith who had stumbled into a world far beyond his backyard. The weight of impostor syndrome was real, pressing down on me amid the crowd of luminaries.

Over the years, my relationship with Milan had deepened through professional stints with British fashion label Boxfresh and extensive engagements with Sportswear Company, known for its revered labels such as C.P. Company and Stone Island. My role at Luxottica required me to visit Milan between three or four times a year, each trip further entrenching my ties to this beautiful city.

Yet, despite these frequent visits and the high-profile events I attended, I never shared these experiences with my friends back in Sydney. Reflecting on it now, I wonder about that silence. Perhaps the stark contrast between my roots and the dazzling world of Milan held me back. Maybe I feared that sharing these stories would create a distance between myself and those I grew up with, or perhaps my struggle was with feeling like an outsider, even as I navigated these strangely unique circles.

How would my mates back in Penrith ever believe this? Amid Milan's elite, as the crème de la crème mingled, I fixated on a D&G knife and fork set, gold-plated and gleaming under the chandelier's light. I pocketed the cutlery in a moment that now feels absurd and revealing. At the time, it felt like I was securing tangible proof of my presence in this opulent world — a bizarre souvenir to validate my experience to friends who knew me as the lad from a far simpler place.

Today, those stolen utensils are nowhere to be found. I'm not even sure I ever shared that surreal night with anyone. Perhaps impostor syndrome held me back, a nagging doubt whispering that I didn't truly belong amid such extravagance. That night taught me about the complexities of belonging, no matter how glamorous the setting might be.

# INSIGHTS

Impostor syndrome is a psychological phenomenon that strikes many of us, particularly in unfamiliar or high-stakes environments. Standing amid the glamour of the Dolce & Gabbana event, I felt it acutely—the sense of being a fraud, perilously close to exposure. My impulse to swipe that D&G cutlery set might seem irrational, but it underscores the lengths to which we will often go to validate our place in worlds we feel unprepared for. This turmoil isn't confined to the overtly unqualified; it seeps into the psyche of even the most skilled among us, casting long shadows over our achievements.

Impostor syndrome isn't merely a fleeting feeling; it's a complex interplay of self-perception and external expectations. Many people navigate this labyrinthine emotional state in their careers and personal lives, revealing that sometimes, our most instructive moments come wrapped in the bizarre.

Growing up in Penrith during the eighties and nineties, and especially the latter, was to live in a town pulsing with the unique rhythm of suburban Australia. During the nineties in Penrith, optimism and gritty realism were mixed. The streets echoed with the sounds of iconic bands, from the grunge of Nirvana to the pop beats of the Spice Girls, shaping a generation teetering on the cusp of the digital age. The youth dressed in a nostalgic wardrobe of denim and daring patterns, influenced by brands such as Billabong and Jag, mixing bold prints and flannel.

Penrith was a town full of opportunity but not without its hardships. It was a place where the concept of men being stoic — where 'men were men', as the saying went — often overshadowed the need for emotional support. When mistakes occurred, people didn't softly gloss over them but pointed them out with a harsh clarity that could be as grounding as it was tough. The people, however, were genuine — salt-of-the-earth types who you knew would always have your back, even if their methods were rough around the edges.

Despite my hometown's camaraderie and down-to-earth authenticity, growing up there sometimes felt constricting. Dreaming big in a small town often meant facing the reality that those dreams could be quickly clipped by well-meaning realism or the small-town fears of failure. Many of my peers fell into the usual vices, drinking and smoking weed, activities I missed due to being wrapped up in cricket. For all its charms, Penrith was also a place where minor missteps could derail major aspirations.

Amid this backdrop, everyone needed a tribe, a group of people to belong to, and I found mine. We were a tight-knit group, as close today as we ever were, but one person stood out, cutting through the norm with his daring to be different — Webby. His spirit and audacity drew us together and pushed us to see beyond the boundaries of our town. Webby was not just a friend but also a catalyst for imagining what could be, a stark contrast to the often stifling atmosphere of small-town expectations.

Webby, my snowboarding adventure bestie from chapter 3 and now a lifelong friend, made me feel invincible growing up. Hopefully, we all have that friend! Where I was cautious, he was fearless. Where I questioned, he leapt. Dirt bikes, rugby, impromptu dance-offs — Webby was always in the centre, with a laugh that could fill a room and a heart that seemed to glow. His bravery wasn't loud or boastful; it was quiet, steady and fiercely loyal.

I tried to keep pace with him. My first foray into rugby league? I lasted all of six minutes. My attempt at barroom valour? A mere eight seconds. But here's the thing: Webby never judged. He had this extraordinary ability to make you feel like the bravest person in the room, even if your idea of bravery was simply showing up.

Webby taught me one of the most invaluable lessons of my life: having the courage to be myself. He was a grounding force in a world that constantly screamed for you to be something else, something more mainstream, something different. He was a mirror reflecting not who you should be but who you already were. And that was enough — more than enough.

When I think of Penrith in the nineties, I don't just think of the music that served as our life's soundtrack or the fashion we wore; I also think of the community we built, the friendships we forged, and the people like Webby who made me who I am. It was more than a time and a place; it was a chapter in our lives that shaped the stories we would go on to tell. And in my account, Webby isn't just a character; he's my cornerstone.

I often think about the Gold restaurant in Milan! I contemplate the distance between Penrith and Gold in Milan, how I managed to get there, and the reason behind my invitation. Through time, I have grown to know that my invitation that night was not by mistake, and I was just as deserving as Ronaldo to be there. If I had my time again, I would have leaned into him, congratulated him on his career and asked him about his day, rather than assuming he was too important. When impostor syndrome is at play, we wear a costume that doesn't quite fit. (Oh wait, that might have been my Oxford suit!)

I don't like feeling uncomfortable. It hurts — not just in the moment but after, too. I now look at discomfort in a different light, however. I grew to understand that displacement was a sign. It forced me to confront the stark contrast between my past and present. It made me question who I was and where I came from but, more importantly, it made me understand that my background was not a limitation — it was a foundation. I started to see my hometown as a launching pad for bigger things.

# INSIGHTS

The work that truly matters doesn't come with a guaranteed outcome. You can pour your heart and soul into an endeavour, but you can never be sure how things will turn out. Don't lose heart, however—the person you want to be is often hidden in the cracks of discomfort in tiny moments of uncertainty.

Uncertainty is unsettling. We all crave a sense of control, to know before we leap. But here's the thing: uncertainty doesn't equal risk.

When discussing uncertainty, I'm talking about a spectrum of outcomes. It's like throwing a dart at a board—you might hit the bullseye or land somewhere in the outer rings. But the key is you're still on the board.

Risk implies the possibility of serious negative consequences, such as losing something valuable or getting hurt. Uncertainty is different. A high school student who applies to several schools that match their academic profile, for example, might prefer to know which ones will say yes. But the odds of getting in somewhere are high. That's uncertainty, not risk.

Don't let the potential discomfort of uncertainty holds you back. You may find yourself hesitating because the future might not match the specific outcome you've fallen in love with. But that's not a good enough reason to play it safe.

As leaders, creators and individuals, we need to ask ourselves whether we are genuinely facing risk or just uncomfortable with an uncertain outcome.

It takes guts to navigate the unknown. But if you let the fear of uncertainty stop you from taking action, you'll miss countless opportunities to make a real difference.

So embrace the uncertainty. Lean into the discomfort. Life is about having the courage to show up. Let the discomfort fuel your fire and guide your way. The most extraordinary adventures and meaningful connections often start in the places you least expect. And the real magic happens when you learn to see your story and background as a source of strength rather than a limitation.

Looking back, I realise that night in Milan was a turning point. It taught me to embrace the full spectrum of my experiences, find strength in my roots and reach a little higher. It showed me that the path to success isn't always a straight line but can also be a winding road filled with unexpected detours and revelations.

Even when seemingly lost among celebrities and genius minds, I now know I am no imposter. I deserved to be there. The invitation to that exclusive event was not a clerical error but an acknowledgement. It was a nod to the hard work I'd put in, the dreams I had chased, and the curiosity that had driven me to ask questions and make decisions.

Over time, I've realised that the stories I was most uncomfortable sharing were often the ones that made me who I am. The Dolce & Gabbana knife and fork may be lost, but the lessons remain. They've significantly shaped my understanding of success, purpose and myself.

◊◊◊

> **In design, the definition is pivotal: it transforms broad, unwieldy problems into specific, solvable challenges.**

In design, the definition is pivotal: it transforms broad, unwieldy problems into specific, solvable challenges. This is a process of deliberate focus, honing in on the heart of what needs resolution. My initiation into design thinking began in 2009. Over the following decade, I applied its principles to various brands, businesses and projects, shaping products and services with a designer's eye.

I then realised I could apply these design thinking strategies to myself. In that instant, I shifted the focus inward, no longer viewing myself as just another project but as an individual deserving of the same meticulous attention.

This self-reflective journey continues today, and remains an ongoing process — constantly evaluating and realigning my core values with my life's purpose. I'm continually rediscovering my 'why'.

In business, articulating this 'why' is easier, a little more black and white. When we created Reny, we knew we needed to prioritise real-world insights over traditional market research or focus groups. Sure, client input is valuable, but it often comes with preconceived notions about what a product should be. So, rather than relying solely on that, we go directly to the source: the people who will use the product. Only by observing user interaction can we truly understand what works and what doesn't. This approach is fundamental to our design philosophy, guiding us in creating genuine products.

Life can be even trickier. It's hard to go it alone and, sure as shit, everyone will have some advice on how you should live it. (Goodness! I am writing a bloody book about it.) But you have to define what you want — and not at the surface but down deep, the things that shape you, the good stuff.

We go through life accumulating experiences, skills, relationships and labels. That's a lot of 'data points'. Definition asks us to sift through these, remove the noise and focus on what matters. We identify core needs and challenges — in this case, our own!

Applying the design process to yourself helps you to move beyond surface-level labels and dig deep into your values, passion and purpose. By defining what makes you tick, you can align your actions and decisions with your authentic self. In this way, self-design focuses on a life lived intentionally and creatively.

What I am diving into here is the power of redefining your view of the world. You can push back against societal norms that confine you to rigid boxes and stifle creativity. You can refute those limiting beliefs that can arise from doubt.

If you approach life as a design challenge, the naysayers and doubters are simply part of the research. They are not the arbiters of what can or cannot be achieved. Creativity teaches us to strip back to the essence. Personal growth teaches us to focus on what we believe is essential, not what society or our immediate environment says is the limit.

> **If you approach life as a design challenge, the naysayers and doubters are simply part of the research.**

When sharing ideas, benchmark them against your values and capacities, rather than someone else's definition of 'real-world limitations'. The real world is as broad as our imagination and as deep as our willingness to delve into it.

Your journey, struggles, community, resources, knowledge, friend circle and imposter feelings are the 'problems' you've defined in your life's designs. These definitions empower you to challenge the very concept of what your 'real world' is, replacing it with a world sculpted by your values, beliefs and aspirations. As Coco Chanel argued, 'The most courageous act is still to think for yourself. Aloud.'

Life is often just a collective agreement, and agreements can be rewritten. If you're looking for one reason 'why it might work', let it be this: because you dared to define it differently, and you dared to begin.

# INSIGHTS

Creativity thrives in the unexpected. Often, the biggest breakthroughs come from those surprising moments that catch you off guard. Detours and chance encounters can offer the most valuable insights.

Know your worth as a creative, but remain open to surprises. Instead of viewing unexpected twists as setbacks, see them as new opportunities. When you allow the unexpected to lead the way, you might just unlock your next big idea.

So, don't resist surprises—embrace them. They could be the spark you've been searching for.

# CHAPTER 6

# SLIM YOUR WALLET

Stripping away distractions to focus on what matters

I remember hearing Tinker Hatfield, one of my favourite shoe designers, say in an interview, 'I don't know if I have a legacy, but I will say that I'm proud of the fact that I'm from a small town in a small state and I've had more than a small impact'. This really resonated with me. I always wanted to leave a mark and Penrith, far from the rolling waves of any beach, simmering in Greater Western Sydney under the intense heat of a relentless sun, was my small town. Penrith was all about football and cricket. Yet, amid this typical suburban sports culture, I harboured a growing fascination with the ocean. It starkly contrasted my reality—although my childhood was filled with daydreams of distant oceans, I rarely experienced sandy toes and salty air.

As the allure of cricket waned, my obsession with surfing grew. Despite years of effort, however, my surfing skills weren't making any waves. Whether I tried shortboards or longboards, my surfing was never graceful. I bumbled and stumbled through each session, yet I stuck with it. I wasn't focused on increasing prowess or performance; after three decades of surfing, I can candidly admit I'm still absolutely crap. But that never really mattered.

For me, surfing became about immersion in something greater than myself, a fleeting yet profound connection with the vast ocean. It offered a rare escape into a sanctuary where the simple, rhythmic sounds of waves drowned out the relentless pings of screens and phones. Standing unsteadily on my longboard in those moments, I found a sense of belonging and tranquillity that Penrith's sports fields could never match.

In the late nineties, Nicola and I made our home at Manly in Sydney, where the ocean dictated the start of each day. My routine was simple yet profoundly satisfying: wake up, peer out to assess the waves and, more often than not, feel the call of the surf pulling me towards the water.

One morning stands out vividly in my memory, though not for reasons I boast about. The waves at Queenscliff Beach, at the northern headland of Manly Beach, were picture-perfect, curling and crashing like images lifted straight from a surfing magazine. With only four surfers out in the line-up, I did wonder if I was missing some crucial information. But the allure of the waves was too strong for me to consider it for long, and I charged towards the surf. (As a sidenote, I always love how we surfers sprint that last stretch to the water — watching surfers run down the beach as if the waves or the day were fading is universally funny! It's as if surfers are all suddenly kids again, racing each other to be the first to dive in.)

I reached the line-up of four guys feeling lucky and ready to go. One of the guys was waving me away. *Yeah, right? There is no chance, buddy, that you are getting these waves all yourselves.* I was, however, confused by the insane crowd of surfers 300 metres to my right on a shitty right-hander. Then came a shout. A warning? *No, just regular surf talk,* I thought. As I confidently paddled into what I believed was my wave, one guy called me a fuckwit, which felt a bit harsh — and then a voice over the loudspeaker boomed, drowning the sound of the crashing waves. Suddenly, the realisation hit: I was the uninvited, clueless intruder amid a World Qualifying Series event.

The vast ocean suddenly seemed tiny. With all eyes seemingly on me, each paddle back to shore felt like an eternity, my every stroke haunted by distant echoes of laughter from the shore. I briefly contemplated an escape route to Freshwater Beach (the family-friendly beach north of Manly).

With its vastness and unpredictability, the ocean has always taught me humility, and that beach blunder still makes me laugh. However, it also reminds me of the close ties between my love for surfing and my professional ventures. My early days saw me mingling with brands that sported some … 'unique' names, such as Buttnaked and Wet Dreams. Yep, I got a few raised eyebrows there! Later, my professional landscape shifted, and I worked with heavyweights such as Oakley, Arnette, Electric, Patagonia, VonZipper and Billabong.

◊◊◊

In 2019, the picturesque coastline of Wollongong became the proving ground for an innovative research initiative that I was privileged to join. The project, hosted by the University of Wollongong, and led by two of the most intelligent and inspiring humans I have ever worked with – Dr Leo Stevens and Dr Marc in het Panhuis – aimed to blend the time-honoured art of surfboard design with the precision of modern technology. (I could dedicate a whole chapter to Leo and Marc's work, and I encourage you to search online to understand the complexity of their thinking better.) Leo and Marc introduced a groundbreaking tool: a 3D-printed surfboard fin fitted with a microchip to gather real-time performance data. This fusion of art and science promised to challenge and expand our traditional understanding of surfboard dynamics.

The core of this research was straightforward yet revolutionary: utilising tech-enhanced fins to test and refine the theories held by seasoned surfboard shapers. Our goal was to align the shaper's design intent with the board's actual behaviour in the water. However, as we collected data, a surprising pattern emerged. We saw a significant discrepancy between the shapers' predictions and the boards' performance metrics. This divergence prompted a broader inquiry, incorporating feedback from professional surfers, who found their perceptions at odds with the empirical data.

Historically, surfboard shaping has been an art form guided by intuition and experience. Iconic brands such as McTavish have relied on inherited wisdom, crafting boards based on feeling, feedback and instinct. From the stable single fin to the agile twin fin and the balanced thruster, each design iteration reflected a blend of artistic creativity and (hopefully) practical functionality.

However, introducing 3D-printed fins equipped with data-collection capabilities marked a pivotal shift. For the first time, we had the means to analyse and enhance surfboard design systematically, with a level of precision that was previously unattainable. This new toolkit allowed designers to craft shapes scientifically, measure speeds and study nuanced manoeuvres, considering variables such as water temperature and wave conditions.

This exploration by Leo and Marc and the University of Wollongong underscores a vital aspect of design — balancing the empirical with the intuitive. As Steve Jobs famously noted, 'Design is not just what it looks like and feels like. Design is how it works.'

The story unfolding through this research is not merely about optimising surfboard performance but also about the broader implications of integrating science into traditional crafts. It challenges us to rethink boundaries and embrace a hybrid approach where innovation meets heritage. This project illustrates the profound impact of questioning and reimagining our tools and methods, propelling a craft steeped in tradition into the future.

# INSIGHTS

Surfboard design, from its origins on the ancient beaches of Polynesia to today's high-tech iterations, has always been about more than functionality—it's also about infusing each board with a soul. This blend of tradition and innovation continues to define the craft, making each surfboard not just a piece of sports equipment but also a testament to the evolving art and science of design.

Sitting at the crossroads of art and science, design and performance, and human craftsmanship and heritage, I found my calling in design. The allure was in creating and connecting—finding that essential middle ground where everything around us is intentionally shaped. This realisation flourished during my time as an innovation consultant, where I saw firsthand that design, while inherently creative, also serves as a vital bridge in all aspects of life.

My understanding of the balance between creativity and logic deepened during an enlightening experience working with Chanel. I once had the privilege of listening to Chanel's international brand manager, who spoke with genuine passion and conviction about the legacy and ethos of the brand. He shared a compelling anecdote about the founder and namesake of the brand, Coco Chanel: every morning, as she prepared to leave her house, she would pause at the mirror and remove one accessory. Whether it was a piece of jewellery or a scarf, this subtraction was her ritual, embodying the philosophy that simplicity often speaks volumes. Chanel's 'less is more' approach isn't just a fashion statement—it's a strategic principle. In a world where businesses often focus on adding more rules, products and services, Chanel excels in the discipline of removal, a tradition Coco set in her Parisian days. Humans are very good at adding, but we are not that good at removing. Maybe the process of removing is just as important as the process of addition.

While all my time spent working with Chanel was inspiring, my last little catch-up with the brand, this time in Milan, was the most bizarre. Influence and inspiration are universal languages, yet sometimes they can be lost in translation during critical moments.

In 2006, I found myself back in Milan, a city I had come to know well through frequent business trips. The constant travel meant sacrificing time with loved ones for interactions with business contacts. While the exposure to diverse cultures and cities was invaluable, and despite Milan's charm, after nearly 15 trips, I was eager to explore unseen corners of Italy. However, I was in Milan for Fashion Week.

The trip's highlight was to be an anticipated talk by the legendary Karl Lagerfeld, the creative force behind Chanel since 1983. Lagerfeld was scheduled to address the gathered business leaders and unveil the new Chanel collections. My access to this exclusive event came courtesy of an old friend, Ed — a brand manager with a passion for seventies culture and modernist design, and a connection from my days with Stone Island.

On arriving at the venue, set up for about 100 attendees, I immediately secured a translator headset, eager to hear from Lagerfeld. The fashion icon soon made his grand entrance, exuding an otherworldly presence with his trademark large collar and distinctive glasses. Expecting to listen to an English translation of his eloquent French, I adjusted my headset and settled in — only to be met with a stream of fluent Mandarin. Confusion swept over me.

As I looked around bewildered, trying to understand the mix-up, I noticed another attendee — an equally perplexed Chinese man — frantically scanning the room. He was experiencing the inverse of my dilemma, listening to an English translation when he needed Mandarin. Amid this linguistic chaos, Karl's voice echoed in the background, his introduction seemingly welcoming us while I sat there, distracted by the hunt for the correct headset.

I eventually made eye contact with the Chinese man, and we quickly swapped headsets without a word, a simple exchange amid the event's formality. I tuned into the English translation to just catch Karl's concluding 'Thank you'. With that, he exited the stage. The man of the hour, Karl Lagerfeld, had come and gone, and all I had managed was a front-row seat to a comedy of errors. Despite the mishap, this brief and bewildering moment with Karl remained a memorable intersection of anticipation and the unexpected — perfectly encapsulating the often unpredictable nature of business and cultural encounters.

Irrespective of my inability to organise a headset in the correct language to listen to the legend Karl Lagerfeld, I've still gained insights on Chanel's design principles and how they influence many of the designers I admire, each bringing their unique blend of art and science. My extensive admiration list begins with Tinker Hatfield and his groundbreaking designs for Nike, which disrupted the athletic footwear market by integrating architectural aesthetics with functional innovation. Also on my list is Yvon Chouinard, even though he doesn't label himself a designer. For me, however, he embodies the essence of thoughtful design in his sustainable approach at Patagonia. Similarly, industrial designers Marc Newson (from Australia) and Yves Béhar (Sweden) fuse technology and design to create products that are both beautiful and beneficial to our daily lives.

Kazuyo Sejima's work in architecture, particularly in blending indoor and outdoor spaces, captures an ethereal balance that challenges our perceptions of physical boundaries. Meanwhile, Vince Frost's graphic design work emphasises clarity and emotional impact, proving that visual communication can be as powerful as it is elegant.

**Design is not merely about the objects we create; it's also about the narratives and experiences we shape through them.**

Each of these designers has influenced my understanding and appreciation of design, not just as a practice but also as a profound approach to interacting with our world. They teach us that design is not merely about the objects we create; it's also about the narratives and experiences we shape through them.

◊◊◊

One designer, for me, will remain my favourite. Over the years and the many brilliant minds I have had the privilege to meet and collaborate with, Andrew Fallshaw stands out not just as my favourite industrial designer and brand strategist but also as a dear friend. Co-founder and CEO of Bellroy, Andrew has consistently demonstrated an unparalleled prowess in melding practicality with aesthetics, transforming everyday objects into elegant, highly functional designs. His design and brand strategy approach is both inventive and deeply inspiring, making him a leading figure in the industry, and a personal inspiration in my creative journey.

We first met in 2009, when the IF (Innovation Forums) talks at Denmark House in Melbourne marked a pivotal moment in my life. I actually met two individuals there who would profoundly influence my trajectory. Firstly, Ben Crowe, a new acquaintance, who would later rise to fame as a mindset and performance coach for champions such as Ash Barty and Steph Gilmore. And then, after the talk, I stepped out for a drink with Andrew Fallshaw. Known to many as the co-founder and CEO of Bellroy, he was 'Ando F' to me, a playful nod to his old Twitter handle. That evening, Andrew handed me a slim, sleek wallet — an embryonic version of what would soon become Bellroy's Slim Sleeve. With a mission encapsulated by the slogan 'Thin your wallet', Andrew, through Bellroy, was set to revolutionise how we carry our essentials.

Going back even further than 2009, our friendship began, interestingly, with a spirited online debate about an article I had written on bottled water. This debate set a foundation of respect and intellectual engagement that led to our meaningful first meeting. Over beers, Andrew unpacked the essence of Bellroy's innovation. By eliminating excess fabric between cards, they had crafted a slimmer wallet and a revolution in functionality. The excitement in his eyes was real, and his belief in the product undeniable.

Andrew Fallshaw stands shoulder to shoulder with industry transformers such as Tinker Hatfield and Yvon Chouinard. By 2022, his vision had propelled Bellroy from a simple prototype to a formidable $330 million empire in the wallet and travel goods sector. But his ambition extended beyond product creation. Andrew envisioned a broader community, coining the term 'carry' to define a new category in consumer goods — one that incorporates bags and travel gear. This vision came to life through Carryology, a blog and curated online store dedicated to exploring the best in carrying gear. This isn't just a promotional platform; the website also encapsulates Andrew's mission to elevate the entire carry sector, fostering a community where innovation thrives and consumer insights drive forward-thinking design.

Witnessing Bellroy's ascent from its nascent stages to a powerhouse has been awe-inspiring. To this day, I treasure that original prototype, a tangible reminder of innovation's humble beginnings.

# INSIGHTS

Bellroy's story is one of humble beginnings, creative thinking, and a deep understanding of design and consumer needs. The name—a clever blend of Bells Beach and Fitzroy, where Andrew lives and works—encapsulates the brand's roots in local craftsmanship and urban sophistication. This synthesis is not just geographical but also deeply ingrained in every product from Bellroy's workshop.

As the mastermind behind Bellroy, Andrew Fallshaw brought with him a rich engineering and creative background when he co-founded the company. His journey through product management and executive roles at Rip Curl provided him with invaluable insights into what makes a product not good, but great. At Rip Curl, he honed his skills in understanding user needs and market dynamics, and crafting functional and stylish products. This experience laid the groundwork for a revolutionary approach to everyday carry items at Bellroy.

The genesis of Bellroy was marked by a desire to redefine how we think about wallets. Traditional wallets were bulky, often crammed with seldom-used items and uncomfortable to carry. Andrew and his team saw an opportunity to innovate and create a functional and aesthetically pleasing product. They began with a simple yet powerful idea: a wallet that could carry essentials in a slim profile without sacrificing style. The end result was a range of wallets that looked good and encouraged users to streamline their lives.

Bellroy's commitment to thoughtful design extends beyond product aesthetics. Each piece is crafted with sustainable materials, ensuring durability and a strict focus on user experience. But perhaps what truly sets Bellroy apart is its human-centric approach. The brand story is imbued with warmth and relatability. Their focus isn't just on selling a product; they're also focused on understanding and improving people's daily lives.

From its modest start, Bellroy has become synonymous with innovation and quality. Its products, ranging from wallets to travel gear, embody a philosophy of practical beauty and efficient functionality. The brand's journey is a testament to the power of starting—with an idea, a prototype and a belief in better design. Andrew Fallshaw's leadership has propelled Bellroy to the forefront of the carry goods industry, and inspired countless others to believe that starting small with the right mix of creativity and practicality can lead to significant, transformative outcomes.

Since my first meeting with Andrew Fallshaw, my fascination with bulky wallets has become a personal crusade. Whenever I met with friends, I couldn't help but zero in on their wallets. It became a fun ritual — snapping photos of the chunkiest wallets I could find and sending them to Ando as part of my unofficial market research. It always felt like I was making a small contribution to what was shaping into a beautifully streamlined brand.

Andrew Fallshaw and Bellroy underscore the profound impact of design in transforming simple ideas into impactful innovations. Starting with a single wallet, Andrew reimagined what everyday objects could be — more functional, stylish and sustainable. This initial design, simple yet purposeful, laid the groundwork for Bellroy to grow into a brand that leads the market and, as a certified B Corp, adheres to the highest social and environmental performance standards. (A B Corp is a for-profit company certified as meeting social sustainability and environmental performance standards by B Lab, a global non-profit organisation.)

This narrative is a testament to the power of starting small and the importance of intention in design. Andrew's journey from a simple idea to a global brand exemplifies how design can bridge functionality with aesthetics, turning ordinary products into extraordinary experiences. It also highlights that the most profound transformations often begin with a single step or idea.

## INSIGHTS

Reflecting on defining moments such as Andrew's brings many insights. Importantly, they highlight the power of recognising and harnessing these pivotal points to refine your creative visions and clarify your goals. These moments invite you to look closely, to find inspiration in life's nuances, and to pursue your objectives with purpose and passion.

Let this story inspire you to see potential in the most straightforward ideas and to remember that significant change often starts with small, deliberate actions. Just as a wallet became a catalyst for innovation, your ideas hold the potential to redefine your path and impact the world.

This journey of creation is deeply personal yet universally impactful. It involves drawing from your cultural background and experiences to forge a unique path. Imagine designing something that not only serves a purpose but also carries a part of your identity — and then placing that product into the hands of another. This act of creation is about more than meeting a need; it's also about making a connection that transcends the functional aspects of the product.

By embracing this holistic approach to design, you position yourself as a creator and visionary, shaping your destiny, influencing the industry, and touching lives. This is how innovators such as Andrew Fallshaw and Tinker Hatfield have made their mark — not only by crafting innovative products but also by inspiring us to see beyond the immediate to the potential ahead.

Let your creations reflect where you've been and envision where you could go. Let them be a testament to your heritage, experiences and dreams. In this way, the design process becomes a journey of self-discovery and profound influence, where every line drawn and idea formed contributes to an imagined and tangible future.

## INSIGHTS

Creativity thrives not in complexity, but in simplicity. When you clear away the clutter and focus on what truly matters, creativity has the space to flourish. You don't need to keep adding more ideas and can instead focus on refining what's already there until its essence shines.

Take a moment to simplify your thoughts, your workspace and your process. This isn't about losing depth; it's about cutting through the noise that clouds your vision. The clearer your focus, the stronger your creativity becomes.

Simplify to amplify.

# PART III

# CONNECTIONS: EXPLORATION

Where ideas collide, connections are made, and creativity is pushed beyond the familiar

Some of my biggest breakthroughs came when I let myself explore without a clear destination. Creativity thrives when we're open to connecting the dots in unexpected ways. Whether in design, strategy or life, the real magic happens when we dare to step beyond the obvious. The more I explored, the more my creative confidence grew. I realised that creativity isn't about having the right answer; it's about discovering new perspectives.

# CHAPTER 7

# DAYLIGHT ROBBERY (BY A LITTLE OLD LADY)!

Seeing creative connections where others see chaos

On an early morning in December 2003, London greeted us with its characteristic chill—a biting cold that somehow sunk through all our layers. A misty fog covered the city as the cobblestone streets shimmered in the light of street lamps, attempting to brighten the gloomy winter morning as double-decker buses rumbled. Nicola and I had become frequent travellers to London from Sydney, making the journey almost quarterly for work and family visits. This trip was to spend time with family and meet with our London-based business partner, Boxfresh, and clothing and footwear brand.

As owners of a start-up, we were struggling financially. Most recent Christmases had been pretty lean — and this one was looking especially so, with a nine-month-old baby in tow. Let's just say pockets were far from bursting. I had gone into Soho, in London, alone and wanted a quick bite before a meeting, so I found an ATM. Due to the winter chill that had the city in its icy grasp, I had to fumble off my mitten just to enter my PIN. (I only removed my right-hand mitten—an essential detail in this story.)

Here's the thing: in Australia, I'd punch in '20', and the ATM would kindly ask for confirmation, to which I would press OK, and the ATM would dispense $20. In London, though, at least back then, the machine had no time for niceties—you hit 20, and it just coughed up the cash. Unfortunately, however, my freezing-clumsy fingers hit '200' instead of '20'. Immediately, the ATM ejected the 200 pounds in ten lots of £20s.

I took them in my *gloved* left hand (notice the vital detail), slightly confused as to what I was doing with £200 in my hand, as I waited patiently for the receipt to spit out. As I stood waiting, cash in my left gloved hand, right hand, ungloved, waiting for the receipt, something strange happened. My money vanished from my left hand. It seemed to completely disappear—but I didn't feel it disappear due to the glove. Unpanicked, I patted myself down and checked my pockets. Then I checked the ground. And then, after 5 or 6 seconds, I became concerned. *What the fuck have I just done with £200?*

That is when I noticed her for the first time. A little old lady was standing right next to me, staring at me and clutching a fist full of cash. She was thumbing through it like a bank teller.

I was in disbelief. The elderly woman, ballpark 80ish, standing within arm's reach, frail in appearance, possibly even homeless, was thumbing through the £200 like a seasoned card dealer. As our eyes met, she looked me straight in the eye, smiled, turned around and walked off. The message was clear: 'Your move.' My mind started playing immediate tricks on me. Was this a coincidence, or was I just robbed by an 80-year-old homeless woman who'd played me as a fool? Yep, that is precisely what happened. An old lady in London robbed me. In broad daylight. Robbed!

After she flashed a smirk and walked off, I saw her slot the money in her left pocket. This was a master at work. Resolute, I knew I had to retrieve my money. Thus began a most peculiar chase through the icy and twisted streets of London — me, a young man, in low-speed pursuit of an elderly woman. It was less of a sprint and more of a determined shuffle, the scene's absurdity compounded by the frigid December air nipping at my heels.

I can almost hear your incredulous reactions urging me to take back what was mine. But consider the spectacle: here I was, chasing someone's grandmother through Soho, my every attempt at retrieval thwarted by her cunning. At one point, driven by desperation, I reached for her jacket pocket, only for her to scream — a sharp, piercing sound that stopped briefcase business people in their tracks. They stared, some shocked, others amused, at the unfolding drama. I looked like the robber here — I was the one stalking her. I was a frustrated ball of anxiousness, wanting to tackle the old lady to the pavement. I considered picking her up and running to a laneway; maybe I could muffle her. Perhaps I could do nothing?

Whenever I managed to catch up, she'd flash a cheeky smile and whisper something indiscernible. Her lips moved as quickly as her feet, taunting whispers lost to the city's hustle. The situation was not only ludicrous but humbling. In a moment of ridiculous diplomacy, I saw a police officer on the outskirts of Covent Garden, eating an oddly long baguette. I frantically ran to him for help. 'Excuse me, sir, a little old lady has robbed me. Can you help?' He continued to eat his baguette while pointing in her direction with a grin. 'Quick,' he told me, 'she's getting away' as she shuffled around a corner. Again, no help!

The chase continued, each of her winks and elusive comments amplifying the absurdity. How could I, a 28-year-old man, publicly confront an 80-year-old woman without turning the situation into a spectacle? Negotiations failed, even as I half-joked about splitting the money. She outmanoeuvred me at every turn, her seasoned wit leaving me frustrated and in an odd sort of admiration for her.

I was stuck in an ethical quandary, robbed by circumstance with no apparent way out. How could I reclaim what was mine without crossing a moral line? She had me cornered, figuratively and literally. I was outplayed, outsmarted and out of options.

I resigned myself to the loss and, though it stung my wallet, I couldn't help but admire her audacity and survival instinct. I trailed behind her for at least 20 minutes, observing as she navigated the streets cunningly. In her unique way, she survived, thriving on her wits. Eventually, I offered her a smile with a mix of resignation and respect. It was similar to the silent acknowledgement exchanged between truckers passing in the night — a mutual nod that spoke volumes.

You might wonder, 'Ben, what does being pickpocketed by a senior citizen have to do with innovation and creativity?' Let me explain — in another roundabout way.

If you've seen the classic Australian film from 1982 *The Man from Snowy River*, you likely remember the scene towards the end when the stallion, the 'Colt from Old Regret', finally gets rounded up by Jim, the 'Man from Snowy River'. The colt looks at Jim and nods, seemingly acknowledging that his attempts to escape were, ultimately, futile against Jim's determined pursuit. Watching the film, I saw this as a moment of surrender and recognition — recognition of each other's capabilities and tenacity. That was somewhat like the silent exchange between me and the old lady. My nod carried respect for her clever tactics, while hers — though I could sense a mix of humour and arrogance — seemed to acknowledge a battle well-fought.

I was outsmarted by a woman who, while maybe not morally upright, was creative and brave. She found an opportunity and exploited it right under my nose. It was her way of 'doing business', surviving in a harsh environment. And while I didn't condone her methods, she was finding her way.

> **Choosing how to make your mark in a world of opportunities is entirely up to you... Everyone can be innovative in their own right.**

Choosing how to make your mark in a world of opportunities is entirely up to you. You could be like that crafty old lady—keen, nimble and opportunistic. But, hopefully, you'll channel those attributes into more socially responsible avenues.

The point is that everyone can be innovative in their own right. You don't have to run a tech start-up or be a digital disruptor. Sometimes, innovation comes in more modest forms—seeing an opening others don't, solving a problem others can't, or delivering value in a way others haven't considered.

## INSIGHTS

A common thread running through my work is *things*. I design things, sell things and make things. When we become obsessed with the things we create, we have to maintain a delicate balance—between form and function, but also between innovation and responsibility. Over time, I've reflected on my connection with the things I love and buy, now as a middle-aged man, and why.

As I've grown older, I've developed a deeper appreciation for the handmade. While I still love the role technology plays in shaping the things we use daily, my approach to buying has evolved, becoming more intentional. I no longer give in to instant gratification, and instead focus more on understanding the impact of my purchases on the planet and humanity.

I used to buy a new phone with every release, for example, chasing the latest and greatest. Now, I wait three to four years until the technology no longer serves me or my business. Only then does an upgrade make sense. This shift in mindset reflects a broader understanding of sustainability and the importance of making thoughtful choices.

I now want to ensure the things I bring into my and my family's lives are meaningful and sustainable. This perspective also shapes how I design, create, live and interact with the world around me.

Creativity, like design, is often misunderstood. People think of both as pathways to creating beautiful art or products. But, in reality, they are about anticipating the future and shaping the world we want to live in. At its core, creativity is simply problem-solving. Design, however, carries a lot more weight.

Around 80 per cent of the environmental impact of a product is defined at the design phase (identified in the 2002 Design Council Annual Review). This reality underscores the urgent need for designers to comprehend their work's impact on the future. Design is not just a tool for meeting human needs; it is a platform for considering the broader implications of those needs. What do people do with the things we create? Single-use plastic is a poignant example of how human-centred design, in its pursuit of convenience, inadvertently created one of the most significant inconveniences of our time.

Human-centred design is not a static concept. It, too, needs to evolve. It should transcend the products we create for people and account for the impact of human behaviours on the places we exist, the communities we live in and the ongoing challenges of the climate we continue to shift.

Designing for *humanity* (rather than humans) feels more important to me, and this then influences my ideas on the role of design. We need to revisit this role and better understand it.

Growing up, my mum was the keeper of all things vintage. She loved design and cherished objects with history. My dad appreciated design, but this appreciation was tied to brands such a Polo Ralph Lauren or Calvin Klein were valued for how they made him look. My mum, on the other hand, valued things for the stories they told. Whether the item was an antique picture or a well-worn piece of furniture, she saw beauty in history. For me, this was where my journey with design began.

An old table Nicola and I bought, which we traced back to the 1940s, provides an example of Mum's love of history and the stories behind things. The table could seat six and had a timeless, Australian heritage design that made it feel earthy and unique. But one detail set it apart — a spot on the table where, over decades, someone had sat repeatedly, wearing down the wood until it bore the mark of countless solitary meals; whoever owned the table before us had certainly lived alone.

My kids would never sit at that worn spot on the table, but my mum? She was drawn to it. She'd run her fingers over the worn surface and say,

'If this table could talk, imagine the stories it would tell.' For her, that mark wasn't a flaw, but a testament to the table's life and memories.

That's what nostalgia is all about. More than simply keeping memories alive, it's about celebrating the narratives embedded in the simplest objects. It's about recognising how these stories help us to remember and feel connected to something larger than ourselves.

> **In a world constantly moving forward, always chasing the next big thing, nostalgia holds an extraordinary power.**

In a world constantly moving forward, always chasing the next big thing, nostalgia holds an extraordinary power. It grounds us, connects us, and reminds us of the value of slowing down and cherishing the moments and objects that have shaped us. When life feels mundane, our stories and memories can reignite that spark of adventure.

In discovering my connection to design, I find myself drawn to the stories we tell about our past and the ones that shape our future. Growing up, my mum did a lot of work for older people within the community—volunteering with her local Meals on Wheels, dropping in to keep them company and hear their stories. She often came home from these visits with gifts, trinkets and crystals. People love to share things because things make people feel, and feeling something is essential.

In some way, the old lady in London who robbed me might have echoed my mum's voice in the back of my mind, urging me to give her space, to let her take the money, to walk away. That experience, as bizarre and unsettling as it was, connected me to a deeper understanding of human nature and the power of empathy.

## INSIGHTS

My mum grew up in Dubbo, a small town in western New South Wales about five hours' drive from Sydney. On any of our longer drives, we would often stop in small country towns and visit thrift stores, rummaging through things from other people's memories and lives—old skis, lamps, mirrors, each item a relic of someone's story. Mum always reminded us of the value these things must have once held for someone. She passed this tradition on to my kids. Miff, Kai, and Pip still have fond memories of rifling through thrift stores with Grandma, discovering treasures and the stories they carried.

My mum fought a lengthy, 16-year battle with cancer. Each year, usually around Christmas, she would gently remind us that it might be her last. She often spoke of life's true essence in those moments: the connections we forge and the stories we share. Mum was quick to share stories from our youth and revisit memories of her parents, Seb and Edie, and her brothers, Tom, Gus, and Perce.

Mum always talked about the old house with a dirt floor she grew up in. Dubbo, with its hot, flat country, was her home. She once wrote a memoir about her childhood, fondly recalling an old tree she used to play under. This tree wasn't just part of the landscape, but also a repository of her cherished childhood memories. She pictured her family under this tree: her dad, mum, brothers, and her best friend, Mary. The tree symbolised the place she always considered home, surrounded by the people she loved.

Mum had a profound connection to the land; her storytelling brought this bond to life. The only possession she ever really wanted was an old Winnebago, as she dreamed of travelling around Australia to see new places. But, deep down, where she truly yearned to be was at home. And to Mum, home was wherever her loved ones were—whether that was Dubbo, Penrith, Sydney, the Blue Mountains or Cooma. Sure, her hometown was Dubbo, but it was never about a place; it was simply where her heart found peace, and that was around her people.

Mum's ambition was unique—fuelled not by a desire for material gain but by a zest for life. As a cancer survivor for 16 years, she lived with the awareness that any year could be her last, and this helped her transform every experience into the best one she ever had. I remember sharing a simple meal of chicken chow mein with her (with her usual request of 'no oil, thanks chef'). She smiled at me and declared it the best thing she'd ever eaten. The next day, we sat on her porch, eating watermelon, and she expressed a similar sentiment—that it was the best watermelon she'd ever tasted.

In 2017, as Mum's long struggle with cancer neared its end, she told me, 'All we have is our memories. Forget about the things; we can't take them with us; focus on the stories and the people'. She squeezed my hand as she said this, a simple gesture that carried the weight of her commitment to family and life.

Mum's journey and her perspective on life continue to guide me. Her emphasis on cherishing memories, nurturing relationships and living a life rich in experiences over possessions is a philosophy I strive to embody.

# INSIGHTS

Redefining success involves shifting our focus from traditional measures, such as financial gain or professional achievements, to a broader, more holistic view. Success is about the depth of our experiences, the positive impact we make and the enduring legacy we leave behind. It's measured in cherished moments and differences made, all indicators of a prosperous life.

Sure, I want to continue to make and have things; things are important. However, we need to be more aware of what we make and the lives they touch. This awareness turns the things we make into powerful objects that can reshape the future.

This perspective on success encourages us to live with intention. It calls for us to infuse our actions and decisions with purpose, ensuring that our work, relationships and life choices have a profound sense of meaning and fulfilment. It's about crafting a life that seamlessly blends passion with purpose, where every moment is lived fully and every action is imbued with personal significance.

Creativity is not a solitary pursuit but a collaborative one. You can find the inspiration and resilience to bring your ideas to life through the richness of your interactions, the depth of your connections, and the courage to embrace new perspectives.

In my diary, I have two secret notes written in messy handwriting in the inside cover of my journal. I can't remember where I found them but they read like this:

*Secret #1 is the biggest one: Have more bad ideas. The more bad ideas, the better. If you work hard to develop but all you discover is bad ideas, some good ideas will slip through sooner or later. This is much easier than the opposite approach.*

*Secret #2 is more important: Be generous. It's much easier and more effective to come up with good ideas for someone else and to adopt a posture of insight and care on their behalf. This generosity lets you off the hook from the burden of needing every idea to validate your worth or prove your genius. It liberates you to focus on serving others and, in doing so, you often discover ideas far more impactful than you imagined.*

*Creativity loves abundance and connection.*

Have you got any ideas?

## INSIGHTS

Creativity isn't just about coming up with new ideas—it's about spotting opportunities where others see none. What's around you that could be reimagined or improved? The most creative people are often the ones who can see what's hiding in plain sight. Challenge yourself to look at a situation from a fresh angle and ask, 'What's the opportunity here that others might miss?'

Creativity often springs up in the most unexpected places. What might look like chaos to others can be the very seed of innovation for you. The trick is to reframe situations and see potential where others see only problems.

Stay curious and keep your mind open to surprises. Embrace the unexpected and let it guide you toward new insights. The next time things don't go as planned, pause and ask, 'What hidden opportunity might be here?'

Creativity flourishes when unpredictability sparks fresh ideas.

# CHAPTER 8

# WATERPROOFED

Breaking through boundaries to explore new
creative possibilities

The fear of being wrong can be one of the most significant barriers
to creativity. The voice that whispers, 'What if it doesn't work?' or
'What if you fail?' can stop ideas even developing. But the truth is
that creativity thrives when we embrace uncertainty, step into the
unknown and allow ourselves the freedom to make mistakes. I love
this quote from author Joseph Chilton Pearce: 'To live a creative life,
we must lose our fear of being wrong'. It took me decades of working
with some of the world's best brands to find my creative confidence to
lean into mistakes, and to know that, sometimes, the best innovations
come from leading in the wrong direction.

In 2005, I entered the Sportswear Company headquarters in Milan,
where Carlo Rivetti was set to unveil the new collection for the fall of
2006. The morning was chilly, but the greenhouse-like showroom,
with light filtering through the glass walls and ceiling, and its polished
concrete floors and elegant mid-century furniture, had a warm buzz.
The displayed clothing from Stone Island and C.P. Company provided a
glimpse into the next season's innovations. At 30 years old, married for
two years and expecting my first child with Nicola, I was eager to take
in Rivetti's announcement. He was a business leader I had met a few
times and admired greatly. That evening, following the announcement,
we had dinner planned in Milan.

My company, which began with long road trips in 2001, had evolved
into the Australian distributor for the Italian men's fashion brands C.P.
Company and Stone Island. We worked tirelessly to crack the code

of introducing these iconic brands to a smaller market. Navigating the challenges of high-end sportswear brands in Australia required a meticulous understanding of their complexities. For years, we devoted ourselves to mastering the delicate balance between upholding their prestigious reputations and catering to our niche audience's unique demands. It was a labour of love more than a financial venture, given the expense of these brands and the limited size of our market.

On a personal level, these partnerships were a masterclass in branding, design and strategy, rooted in decades of history and Italian craftsmanship. That four-year window was a critical period in my business journey, fast-tracking my understanding of building brands and designing with intention and purpose. It shaped my approach to business, and gave me valuable insights into creating something that connects deeply with an audience.

# INSIGHTS

C.P. Company, founded in 1971 by Italian designer Massimo Osti, has a rich legacy rooted in innovative design. Initially named Chester Perry, the brand was renamed to C.P. Company in 1978, following a legal dispute with Chester Barrie and Fred Perry. The brand became synonymous with functional, military-inspired outerwear and groundbreaking fabrics, including the 'Mille Miglia' or 'Goggle Jacket'. This distinctive piece, featuring two clear lenses on the hood and one on the wrist for checking a watch, became an iconic garment that still turns heads today. Designs based on their research into military and workwear uniforms gave their clothing a rugged yet modern appeal, attracting a dedicated following, particularly among Dutch and English football subcultures.

Remarkable achievements in fabric development and garment dyeing techniques marked the brand's journey. Their technologically advanced dyeing laboratory in Ravarino, Italy, was crucial in the company perfecting garment dyeing, and offering a range of unique finishes to clothing. C.P. Company, for example, pioneered the use of advanced materials such as Dynafil TS-70, a protective fabric on a non-rip, non-scratch nylon base, and Chrome, 100 per cent regenerated nylon. Their approach to textile innovation also allowed them to use a single raw material across multiple seasons, enhancing sustainability.

The brand's military-style aesthetic and technical prowess connected strongly with the casual subculture that emerged in the United Kingdom during the 1980s. C.P. Company's collaborations with artists, musicians and other brands also expanded its cultural reach, reinforcing its iconic status in high-tech outerwear. The Mille Miglia jacket, in particular, has appeared on the covers of albums, books and gallery exhibitions, a testament to its cultural significance.

Designer Massimo Osti went on to found Stone Island, an Italian luxury fashion brand specialising in men's apparel, outerwear and accessories, in 1982. Its branding features a nautical star and compass logo on a green, yellow and black badge, symbolising a commitment to functionality and exploration. Initially envisioned as a complementary label to C.P. Company, Stone Island quickly gained popularity in its own right in Europe and Japan throughout the 1980s and 1990s, and expanded into the United States and Canada in the 2010s. The brand became renowned for its signature reflective fabric, innovative dyeing techniques and unique surface treatments.

The brand emphasises technical research, development and manufacturing processes, which have led to innovations such as Raso Gommato (1983), thermosensitive fabric (1987), rubber wool (1987) and reflective fabric (1991). Stone Island's consistent focus on cutting-edge textile innovation resulted in designs that prioritised utility while embracing an anti-fashion ethos, making its garments instantly recognisable.

Stone Island's influence extended far beyond the realm of high fashion. Its bold, practical designs, and especially the compass badge, became emblematic within various subcultures. In the late 1980s, wealthy Italian teens adopted the brand's unconventional fabrics and silhouettes. By the mid-1990s, Stone Island was embraced by English football casuals, further cementing its association with the sport and its hooliganism subculture. This affiliation with football fandom was immortalised in films such as *Green Street* (starring Elijah Wood and Charlie Hunnam) and *The Football Factory* (starring Danny Dyer).

In the 2000s, the brand gained traction in the United States and Canada, primarily through streetwear and hip-hop culture. Stone Island's badge became a coveted status symbol, visible to Milanese youth, athletes and celebrities. British magazine *i-D* noted that 'getting the badge in' helped Stone Island maintain its position as a high-end icon among youth.

*(continued)*

Despite its reputation among football hooligans and streetwear enthusiasts, Stone Island remains a pinnacle of technical apparel innovation, blending functional fabrics with modern silhouettes. The brand's ongoing collaborations with design companies such as Supreme, Nike and New Balance have ensured its continued relevance, merging high-end fashion with street culture in a distinctive way.

In the mid-1980s, Carlo Rivetti took over ownership of C.P. Company and in 1993 also took over Stone Island, renaming the combined activities Sportswear Company. In 2020, Moncler acquired the Stone Island brand for €1.15 billion, further cementing its place in the world of luxury fashion.

Back to that chilly morning in 2005. I was in Milan to meet Carlo Rivetti and the other distributors of the Sportswear Company. Carlo was a visionary—his reputation preceded him as the mastermind who had transformed Stone Island into a powerhouse of cutting-edge fashion. He came from a lineage deeply rooted in Italy's textile industry, and had inherited a legacy of creativity and innovation. Carlo had an unwavering commitment to research and experimentation that pushed the boundaries of what sportswear could be.

He had an announcement that day, and we all gathered around, eager to hear his vision. An unmistakable energy was in the room. With his distinctive style and highlighting his deep understanding of the market, Carlo spoke about the future of Stone Island. He shared how the brand would continue to break new ground by blending functionality and innovative design in a way only he could envision. The plan was clear: maintaining Stone Island's unique identity while expanding its reach and reinforcing its reputation as a global leader in high-performance fashion.

During the meeting, Carlo Rivetti unveiled something genuinely groundbreaking: garment-dyed Gore-Tex. Gore-Tex itself hadn't spearheaded this innovation; rather, the Sportswear Company had. Under Carlo's leadership, the design team had pushed the boundaries of textile technology in a bold and understated move. This was the first time in history that Gore-Tex would be available in bold colours. Before this, Gore-Tex was black, blue and grey. Thanks to these announcements, we could now see it in bright orange or yellow.

In an industry that often leans towards loud declarations of innovation, Carlo's approach was refreshingly different. He believed true innovation does not require flashy announcements; it connects through its impact and adoption within the industry.

He was confident that while others might attempt to imitate this pioneering technique, his approach's originality and ingenuity would stand unmatched. This philosophy of quiet confidence underscored Carlo's vision for sustained influence and growth in the high-end fashion sector.

I have to admit, back then, Carlo's announcement seemed inconsequential. I couldn't grasp its significance at first — so he'd added some colour to Gore-Tex. Was that it? Before I fully appreciated the complexities of design, the processes all seemed straightforward, as if the garments we wore magically appeared. But during that meeting, I came to understand the immense effort involved. Carlo talked us through the intricate process of marrying science, design and engineering to create a product that would revolutionise Sportswear Company's offerings and transform Gore-Tex's collaborations across the industry. The impact of that innovation was far-reaching, affecting brands connected to Gore-Tex in ways unimaginable at that time.

Reflecting on that moment, I recognise its profound impact on my professional path. That meeting transcended a mere introduction to a fashion innovation; it was a deep dive into strategic branding and humility. Initially, I couldn't see the significance of Carlo and his team's work in garment-dying Gore-Tex. Yet now, every mountain trek reminds me of that day's lessons. My vibrant yellow Patagonia jacket, my daughter's cheerful blue Roxy, and my wife's striking Burton owe their existence to the pioneering work I witnessed in 2006. This experience taught me to appreciate the complex human ingenuity behind every product and the meticulous effort required to bring a simple idea to life.

## INSIGHTS

It still dawns on me as strange that I would find myself in these rooms and in places such as Carlo Rivetti's Gore-Tex announcement, my past at the time still rooted in Penrith and cricket pitches. As I ventured out into the world, I took a lot of years to settle into being present with the idea that I deserved

*(continued)*

to be there. In the early years, I would look around a room at all the successful people running successful companies worldwide and wonder how I got there. Do I need to quote Steve Jobs again here? 'You can't connect the dots looking forward; you can only connect them looking backwards'. But for me at 30, looking back, I saw an eight-year battle with trying to fumble my way, essentially uneducated, into building a business that was building brands. Somehow, I ended up forging out a multimillion-dollar company—but if you had asked me to explain how, I couldn't have explained it back then.

As I write this, I can look back and connect the dots. I have done the work and understand why I was in the room that day—because I showed up, said I could do it and cared enough to dream. During certain chapters and periods in my life, I stopped dreaming, or my dreams shifted away from me to my kid's dreams. My path swayed from chasing these dreams because they didn't match my values then. But I always found my way back.

It's easy to forget the human ingenuity behind each product we rely on, and overlook the years of research and development that made the product possible. We must remember that everything we use began as an idea in someone's mind—a concept born, refined and courageously brought into reality. While ideas are freely formed, their realisation often demands significant cost and dedication.

Between 2016 and 2020, I spent around 100 days each year in the mountains, exposing myself and my family to the harsh weather conditions and cementing my trust in Gore-Tex. Even my youngest, Pip, from the tender age of three, specifically requested her Gore-Tex jacket before hitting the mountains—it was extraordinary. This fabric didn't just protect us from the elements; it wove itself into the fabric of our mountain adventures, becoming as essential to our snowboarding stories as the snow itself.

Before the invention of Gore-Tex, options for materials that could protect against harsh weather existed but were far from perfect. Waxed cotton was durable but uncomfortably heavy. Vinyl, while waterproof, was akin to wearing a sauna suit, trapping sweat inside. Seal intestine, though ingeniously used by the Inuit First Nations peoples in the Artic regions of North America, was impractical for broader production.

Carlo Rivetti's design wisdom is echoed in Gore-Tex's journey. Like Carlo, Gore-Tex has let its innovation do the talking, from accidental discoveries such as expanded PTFE (resulting in an incredibly strong, microporous material) to industry-changing collaborations. It's a reminder that true pioneers don't need to boast; their work speaks volumes and leaves an indelible impression on industries and markets.

As you may have gathered, my passion for Nike runs deep, ignited by iconic models such as the original Blazer 77 and the Bruin, famously worn by Michael J Fox in 1985's *Back to the Future*. These shoes graced countless other eighties movie screens, and symbolised a broader culture of innovation and style that Nike continually championed. This admiration extends to the genius of Tinker Hatfield, designer for Nike, whose designs reshaped how we think about athletic footwear. This same reverence for groundbreaking creativity and enduring impact informs my equal commitment to Gore-Tex.

Much like Nike, Gore-Tex isn't just a brand I admire; it's a significant chapter in my narrative. This relationship began somewhat unassumingly but now symbolises a cornerstone of innovation that aligns closely with my professional ethos. At first, I underestimated the impact of Gore-Tex, viewing it as just another functional material. Over time, however, I came to recognise it as a paradigm of how quiet innovation can drive substantial change — offering solutions that are not only effective but also ethically grounded and sustainable. My journey with Gore-Tex reflects a broader ambition: to achieve quiet but profound innovation, solve problems ethically and create lasting value in whatever I undertake.

## INSIGHTS

Gore-Tex, a name synonymous with innovation and resilience in fabric technology, has a story that feels almost destined. It starts humbly, back in 1958, in the basement of Wilbert L Gore and his wife, Genevieve Walton Gore. Together, they founded W. L. Gore & Associates, eventually transforming a simple venture into a beacon of pioneering excellence.

In 1969, Wilbert's son, Bob Gore, was engrossed in researching how to stretch extruded polytetrafluoroethylene (PTFE) into pipe thread tape when he made a remarkable discovery — almost by accident. Previously, the approach involved slowly

*(continued)*

stretching the heated polymer to around 10 per cent of its original size. But on this particular day, partly out of frustration and impatience, Bob tried something different: instead of a gentle, measured stretch, he yanked the heated rod suddenly and forcefully. This abrupt movement resulted in an unexpected phenomenon: the solid PTFE stretched about 1000 per cent, transforming it into a microporous structure comprising about 70 per cent air.

This newly expanded material revealed a unique combination of high strength and porosity, opening up a world of possibilities for the polymer. Bob quickly filed for a patent in 1970, recognising the significance of his accidental breakthrough. Two separate patents would ultimately be issued: one covering the product itself and another detailing the processes used to create it.

Bob didn't stop there. He continued experimenting with different PTFE resins, exploring the potential of stretching the material both one-dimensionally, to produce long filaments, and two-dimensionally, to form durable sheets. Two-dimensional stretching yielded stronger, more porous and more breathable sheets, creating new applications for the revolutionary polymer.

By 1971, Bob was working on laminates that combined the stretched membrane with other materials for increased strength. These efforts culminated in the invention of expanded polytetrafluoroethylene (ePTFE), which is now trademarked as Gore-Tex. This waterproof yet breathable laminate would transform outdoor wear and other applications, demonstrating that, sometimes, the most significant innovations arise from frustration, perseverance and the willingness to try something unconventional.

Bob's discovery illustrates that creativity often strikes unexpectedly, flourishing at the crossroads of persistence and chance. Gore-Tex is a profound reminder of the virtues of patience and the immense potential hidden in unforeseen outcomes. Breakthroughs often arise from the willingness to experiment and the readiness to embrace the unexpected, pushing the limits of what we believe is possible.

Owning a brand and nurturing a great idea is one thing, but knowing how to transform that vision into a thriving company is entirely different. As my fascination with Gore-Tex deepened, I began to appreciate the company's innovative approach—not just in its products but also in the culture and ethos it fosters within the organisation. Their commitment to creativity and innovation permeates every business layer, ensuring that they aren't merely crafting groundbreaking fabrics but also building a culture that champions experimentation, integrity and long-term vision.

**Owning a brand and nurturing a great idea is one thing, but knowing how to transform that vision into a thriving company is entirely different.**

Gore-Tex's organisational structure—a flat lattice model—isn't just unconventional; it's radical in the context of traditional corporate culture. A hierarchical setting features a chain of command, which often means a chain of approval, slowing down the creative process. The lattice model, however, encourages spontaneous and direct communication between individuals. The absence of traditional bosses doesn't mean a lack of leadership; leadership responsibilities are instead decentralised and shared. This disrupts the usual 'wait-for-approval' dynamic and accelerates innovation.

The role of 'sponsors' in this model is also fascinating. Gore-Tex has a mentoring system on steroids. Sponsors in this system don't just give advice; they empower team members to take ownership of their roles. They're more like coaches than managers, helping to identify strengths and weaknesses, set goals, and offer the resources to achieve those objectives. They're less concerned with management and more with guidance, thereby creating a culture of self-management where employees are their own bosses to some extent.

Regarding time allocation for passion projects, this is another layer of genius. People being more engaged and productive when working on projects they're passionate about is common knowledge. But what's less acknowledged is that these 'side projects' often result in some of a company's most groundbreaking work. Consider Google's '20 per cent time', where employees are encouraged to spend 20 per cent of their time working on what they think will most benefit Google. This approach gave us products such as Gmail and Google AdSense. When employees are invested in their work at this level, it's not just a job—it's a calling. This emotional investment forms a fertile ground for divergent thinking, as employees feel they have the space and support to think creatively and take risks.

This structure fosters a culture of collaboration, not competition. In many organisations, employees are pitted against each other, vying for the boss's attention to climb the corporate ladder. Gore-Tex's lattice structure obliterates the ladder. There's no climbing — just connecting. Team members are naturally encouraged to pool their varied skills and insights, leading to more holistic solutions.

This framework allows for creativity and divergent thinking; it actively cultivates employees as part of the company's DNA. It acknowledges that innovation is not a solitary endeavour but a collective pursuit that thrives in an environment free from the restrictions of conventional corporate hierarchy.

Gore-Tex's philosophy on failure was another integral part of its innovation strategy. The concept is an excellent enabler of what you might call 'safe failure', offering employees the latitude to explore and take calculated risks without the dread of significant repercussions. Doing so liberates them from the stultifying fear of making mistakes — often the most critical barrier to creative exploration and innovation.

## INSIGHTS

In conventional settings, failure often has punitive consequences, resulting in a risk-averse culture. In contrast, Gore-Tex's approach effectively decouples the act of failure from the stigma traditionally attached to it. Reframing failure as a learning experience transforms what is usually seen as a setback into an opportunity for iterative development. Each failed experiment becomes a lesson, contributing to a knowledge bank that informs future projects. This is a complete paradigm shift in how we traditionally understand business operations.

This culture of experimentation has contributed to the diversification of their product line, far beyond their initial waterproof fabric. Imagine the audacity to move from outdoor gear material to heart patches. That's not just lateral thinking; it's multi-dimensional thinking. The foundational ePTFE technology unifies these diverse products, but what brings them to life is the freedom and encouragement to stray from the beaten path.

In a society that often measures success by your financial status, resisting such pressures isn't just unconventional — it's radical.

And yet, we've all heard the tales of those earning top dollar but finding themselves trapped in cycles of stress and unfulfilment. Therein lies a potent irony: while money can be counted, measured and deposited, it's often the elusive qualities—such as happiness, purpose and a sense of community—that enrich our lives in ways that can't be quantified.

Interestingly enough, economic data backs this up. Studies have shown that, after a certain point, additional income brings diminishing returns in terms of happiness. So the pressing question becomes this: can we truly afford not to prioritise the things that matter most to us, do the jobs we dream of, and work with purpose?

Business isn't a walk in the park; it's a continual balancing act, especially when you're passionately creative. Some days, the seesaw teeters dangerously, and keeping those metaphorical doors ajar feels like an arduous task. But it's precisely in navigating these challenges that we find our balance — not just keeping the lights on (sometimes just barely) but also fuelling the creative sparks that lead to our most fulfilling work.

This is also why I have Alma-Nac — a little idea lab created for myself without any commercial ideology attached to it. Alma-Nac serves as my sandbox, my (virtual) laboratory for creative experimentation. I'm not concerned about revenue (actually, we don't make any money); instead, I use this lab to focus on my sheer love for design and experimentation. It is my sacred creative space where I can create anything I imagine. Sometimes, I repurpose waste — such as old DVDs and bio-acetate frames (derived from renewable resources such as cotton linters and wood pulp) — and turn them into functional eyewear. It's not a commercial endeavour; it's an exercise in creative agility and authenticity.

This project has taken me on a global journey, connecting me with artisans from Spain, Japan and China. While eyewear remains the cornerstone of my passion brand, Vert, the project has evolved to include a range of other sustainable designs — such as for buildings, shoes, coffee machines and even an un-smart phone with no notification or backlight. It's an ongoing exploration that embodies my commitment to a deeper understanding of design, production and sustainability.

So, while Reny is the main canvas for my life's work, Alma-Nac is my playground — my haven for tinkering, innovating and experimenting, all free from market pressures. It's a tangible manifestation of my curiosity to understand divergent thinking more profoundly. (It might also be a little like your dad's shed, where he used to tinker with the tools in the garden.)

In the business context Reny is based on, which is focused on impact-led design, divergent thinking can be a goldmine. It can drive us to explore radical design solutions, evaluate various user experiences or re-imagine a business model. Similarly, applying divergent thinking in user experience design might lead you to novel ways of increasing user engagement. In contrast, in product design, it could mean experimenting with sustainable materials that no-one else in your industry is even considering.

## INSIGHTS

Creativity thrives on momentum—the driving force that propels an idea into fruition. This flow turns sparks into flames, pushing innovations from concept to reality. When momentum stalls, on the other hand, creativity suffers. Projects can become mired in hesitation or bureaucratic delays, transforming passion into a chore. This stagnation is where potential breakthroughs die, leading to project failures and a broader impact of missed opportunities and unrealised possibilities.

Creative momentum comes from small victories. Recognising each victory, no matter how minor, ensures a continual push towards continuous learning. This prevents projects from becoming bogged down and keeps the creative energy alive.

Time plays a dual role in creative projects. While it can be a luxury that allows for detailed perfection, it's also a ticking clock that can doom a project if prolonged. The longer an idea remains just an idea, the more likely its initial spark will fade.

**Embrace the rhythm of quick successes to sustain momentum and keep your creative journey alive.**

The pace at which you can deliver something tangible often determines how fast you can iterate, adapt and excel. Embrace the rhythm of quick successes to sustain momentum and keep your creative journey alive.

Start small and start now. This makes a lot more sense than starting big and starting later.

You don't have to start perfect. You just have to start.

## INSIGHTS

Creativity isn't just about coming up with fresh ideas or finding the courage to step outside your comfort zone. Real breakthroughs emerge when you dare to challenge norms and venture into uncharted territories. This option is not always the easiest path, but it's where true innovation happens.

Be bold enough to push past boundaries, be ready to adapt and welcome the unknown.

Creative confidence comes from daring to stretch the edges of your comfort zone.

# CHAPTER 9

# INDOOR WHAT?

Stretching your creativity by connecting
the unexpected

For all our charms, the Rennie family has never mastered the art of dancing. I came to terms with this truth during a disco in 1988 — the same year Brisbane dazzled the world with Expo 88. Yet, amid neon lights and buzzing excitement, my brother unwittingly showcased a different spectacle at the Leonay Golf Club's Blue Light Disco.

If you're unacquainted, Blue Light Discos were a phenomenon of the eighties and nineties, held across Australia and linked with the local police as a safe space for kids to socialise, dance and hang out. These events, often bathed in the stark, flashing lights of police strobes, offered a unique backdrop that seemed more suited to a quirky sci-fi film than a teen's dance party. Amid this surreal setting, the image of my brother attempting to dance remains etched in my memory, a vivid tableau of rhythmic challenges that halted me mid-step.

His performance was nothing short of mesmerising. Dubbed the 'white man's overbite', his particular dance style involved an intense concentration that drew his bottom lip under his teeth — a look of focus so severe, it seemed comically out of place on the dance floor. His movements were large and uncoordinated, swinging dramatically from side to side. Each step he took spanned a near metre to the left or right, his body tilting at a precarious 60-degree angle as he transitioned from one side to the other, all while his head bobbed earnestly to Huey Lewis's 'The Power of Love'.

That day marked the day I swore never to dance. Ever. And it took a few years and the power of Cindy Lauper to get me swaying again! (I share more of that story in chapter 16.)

In 1988, World Expo 88 served as a cultural thunderclap heard across Australia as we proudly showcased our quirky Australian culture and heritage to the globe. With Paul Hogan already heralding the charms of our harbours and beaches (and the shrimp on our barbies), the world's eyes were on us. Seized by the excitement, my family decided to experience it firsthand. We piled into Dad's third Ford Telstar, still in its steadfast silver, and set off for Brisbane. Road trips in the eighties were often brutal: sticking to the vinyl seats, grappling with a temperamental aircon that favoured the front, and cringing every time the metal seat belt buckle scalded my skin when I dared to readjust my stuckness! Today, my kids nestled in the family hybrid BMW X5 on trips to the snow couldn't possibly fathom such discomfort. They don't dare utter a word of discomfort with me helming the wheel!

Once we got to Expo 88, we wandered into the dazzling US pavilion, plastered with images of basketballer Magic Johnson and track and field star Carl Lewis. Hidden at the back was a real music studio, an awe-inspiring sight for a 13-year-old me. I glanced at Dad, and he gave me an encouraging look. With an air of confidence and my dad's supportive suggestion — 'You've got this, son, sing your heart out!' — I didn't hesitate. Forking over $50, I stepped into the booth, the producer ushering me in with a brisk, 'Pick a song, son', in his thick Yankee accent. He gave me about eight seconds to pick. Without a second thought, I chose Lionel Richie's 'Dancing on the Ceiling'. 'Hit it!' he commanded again, and in another eight seconds, the studio recording light was glowing red. Just like that, I was belting out tunes in a genuine recording studio. I was doing it, singing; I could feel the energy, my ticket to a new life!

As I walked out, my American friend offered no words of awe; he just handed me a tape. (I hope this goes without saying, but the compact cassette, also commonly called a cassette tape, audio cassette or simply tape or cassette, is an analogue magnetic tape recording format for audio recording and playback.)

Now clutching the tape that contained my potential hit, I spent the day swaggering around the expo, half believing that the crowds recognised the new star among them. I felt famous. This was my time. All I really wanted all day was to return to the car and listen to the tape. I was frustrated that the recording studio hadn't let me hear it from the booth. He simply ushered me out the door as he ushered in the next act. As I left the booth, I asked him if I could listen back to my recording. He replied confidently, 'You sure can, kid. Go buy yourself a Walkman and knock yourself out!'

At the end of a long day of zigging and zagging throughout seemingly every nation on Earth, the Ford Telstar was waiting. We packed in to head back to the hotel.

'Press play, Dad, press play!' I shouted with anticipation as Dad inserted my tape. As we slowly pulled out of the parking spot, the tape began to play and my voice filled the car. It was me singing — and we had it loud, really loud!

As my recorded voice continued, a profound silence fell over the occupants of our car. Slowly, the vehicle pulled to an awkward stop in the middle of the lane, and my dad buried his face in his hands, his body shuddering. Was he okay? My mum was now staring out the window into the sky, her shoulders jumping. Why was no one looking at me? What was happening?

Then, without warning, I heard a snort from my mum, the kind of snort I had never heard before. It was loud, maybe even snot-inducing! Next, Mum had erupted into laughter! My dad, shuddering still, was soon also snorting with tears and laughter; I sat in the back in silence as my version of 'Dancing in the Ceiling' played on. We were certainly not dancing on the ceiling; we were parked, creating a traffic jam. Mum was struggling to catch her breath, while Dad seemed to be having some sort of asthma-induced attack, and couldn't breathe from laughing so hard. Finally, Mum turned to me in the back seat and, with teary eyes, managed to choke out, 'It's good, son, so good. I am so proud of you' — except her words were barely legibly between the tears and laughter!

At that moment, any remnants of my brother's embarrassment from earlier dance debacles seemed avenged by my vocal performance — and the family's reaction, a mixture of humour and affectionate teasing.

◊◊◊

Music has always been the backdrop of my life, charting the highs, the lows, and the moments in between. The opposite is also true — each note of my life has shaped my musical soundtrack. Singing? The answer is always yes, despite my Expo 88 moment. Dancing? Let's just say I'm still haunted by memories of my brother's Blue Light missteps. Over the years, however, I have found myself in some iconic music spots — but none as iconic as the Blue Note in Milan.

Opened in 1981, the Blue Note became more than just a jazz club — it became a legend. Inspired by the bustling jazz scene of New York City, the club captured that same spirit and authenticity, transplanting it into Milan's vibrant cultural fabric. The place has a certain magic. It's small enough to feel intimate, with dim lighting that lets the stage shine and plush seats that invite you to settle in for a night of pure musical indulgence.

At the Blue Note, it's all about the music. You step inside and the rest of the world fades away. The rules are simple: keep your conversations low, let the music lead and give the musicians the respect they deserve. It's a place where every performance is a tribute to jazz legends such as Miles Davis, John Coltrane and Billie Holiday — they've all been honoured here, their spirits lingering in the air in every riff and every improvisational jam.

This isn't just any music venue. It's a cornerstone of jazz history, where the past meets the present, and the future of jazz is forged in real time.

My first night at the Blue Note in Milan followed an afternoon at Bar Magenta, just steps from where Leonardo da Vinci's *The Last Supper* resides. Let's just say this arvo was less about high culture and more about high spirits. Nestled in the heart of Milan, the iconic bar with charming outdoor tables is perfect for soaking in the city's historic atmosphere — one Peroni at a time. That day, I indulged in quite a few, basking under the Milanese sun and losing track of time and beers.

By 6 pm, the world began swaying slightly with each Peroni sip. Laughing off the buzz, I bid farewell to my anonymous drinking companions — whose faces were as blurry as my recollection of that afternoon — and staggered back to my hotel.

Slipping into my room, I found a note tucked under the door. It was an invitation from business colleagues, calling for a night out at the Blue Note. The plan? A night of jazz. My plan was slightly different. I heard 'jazz', and all I could think of was the enthusiasm of my brother's infamous dance moves — left, right, left, right, with the quintessential white man's overbite. Excitement surged through me. *This is it*, I thought. *Tonight, I dance!*

It was only 6.30 pm, but with the night already set and spirits high, I hit the hotel bar for a quick bite and a few more rounds with my mate, Ben, from London. In 2006, at 31 years old, I wasn't exactly the epitome of restraint. Reflecting on those 16 Peronis and Camparis, it's clear they weren't doing any favours for my maturity — or my forthcoming dance skills. I need to add a disclaimer here, and this is important: I didn't know, at the time, what the Blue Note was; all I heard was 'jazz', and all I wanted was to dance. Right, back to the story!

I arrived at the Blue Note on time and greeted my colleagues, ruffling their hair and slapping their backs, hugging them like I had won something.

An eerie hush fell over the crowd as the band struck their first notes. The sudden silence was puzzling — why wasn't anyone talking or even whispering? Compelled to inject some life into the sombre atmosphere, I stood up and started clapping rhythmically to the music. Undoubtedly, the band deserved some appreciation for their flawless performance! Yet my efforts were met with quiet stares and an uncomfortable silence that refused to break.

Fuelled by confusion and misplaced enthusiasm, I loudly expressed my admiration for jazz legends like Coltrane and Otis Redding. I intended to spark some conversation, even some camaraderie. But as the silence stretched, I felt a surge of boldness that could only mean one thing: it was time for the Rennie family dance.

There I was, channelling years of dance floor avoidance into a moment of reckless abandon, strutting side to side with arms flung wide as if alone in my living room. But I wasn't alone; the entire club was watching. Whispers turned to shushes, mild boos emerged from the crowd, and I even spotted a few band members pointing in my direction. *Yes*, I thought, mistaking their gestures for encouragement, *keep dancing, Ben!*

Just as I was getting into the groove, feeling lighter by the moment, reality — in the form of two very polite Italian gentlemen — brought me back to earth. Each took an arm, and before I knew it, I was floating through the crowd, buoyed not by the magic of dance but by the firm guidance of my new escorts. They gently led me to the foyer and kindly asked me to sit. Confused, slightly buzzed, and now seated, I was left to ponder the unexpected end to my jazzy jig. Why had they silenced me? Why the escort out?

As I sat there, the absurdity of the situation dawned on me. The Blue Note wasn't quite ready for the Rennie dance revival.

The manager of the Blue Note approached with discretion that matched the venue's understated elegance. He gently reminded me that I was in one of the most esteemed jazz clubs in the world. 'Here, we sit, listen and deeply appreciate the artistry of the music', he advised, his voice firm yet kind. There was to be no noise — only appreciation.

Could I manage that? I nodded sheepishly and expressed gratitude for the chance to correct my course.

Guided back to my table, I was met with a spectrum of reactions from my colleagues — from amused smiles to slightly disapproving glances. I settled into my seat, took a humble sip of water and let the music sink in. The rest of the evening unfolded beautifully, each note spellbinding and captivating. It turned into one of the most enchanting nights I've ever experienced.

After the performance, I made a point to circle back to the manager and anyone else I might have disturbed, offering sincere apologies for my earlier disruption. It was a night that started with no expectations and ended with a deep-seated appreciation for the music and the discipline of truly being present in a moment of unparalleled creativity.

# INSIGHTS

You know I had forgotten that story from the Blue Note. I love this aspect of writing; it takes me back to places I sometimes forget. That moment at the Blue Note could have been forgotten, but it's still a moment in time that's mine. When I was growing up, writers seemed to create the illusion that they had all the answers. I would look at writers as if they were some kind of oracle. But they are not. They are just sharing words on a page; with time to share, the words find their way to the keyboard. Writers are not oracles. They are just brave.

In the real world, I'm paralysed by fear some days, and not a week goes by without me questioning everything — my decisions, my path, my very existence and my parenting. Our past can be a double-edged sword. It can inform and hinder our future, robbing us of our potential and opportunities.

My mum used to say that everyone has a book inside them. Like many of us, she held dreams close to her heart, some of which she never had the chance to fulfil. One of her dreams was to write a book. I carry her unrealised aspirations as a constant reminder.

Not long after Mum passed, I opened my laptop to write this book.

During Mum's final days, she handed me an umpire's rule book from the indoor cricket centre my parents once owned. It was a small A5-sized book, and was ancient and worn. By the time she handed it to me, Mum had lost her ability to speak. She could only squeeze my hand and gesture.

The little rule book was instantly familiar; I had seen it often over the years. If my brother and I stepped out of line, she would pull it out and read us a quote from it. This could be something that she had written in the book ten years prior, based on a lesson learned from watching adults play sports, sometimes acting like children.

In the 1980s, my parents, early pioneers and entrepreneurs, made their mark in Western Sydney, with their second business venture being an indoor cricket centre (which I also talk about in chapter 2). The first was a sandwich shop in Campbelltown, west of Sydney, which, incidentally, didn't sell many sandwiches and met with a mysterious fate by fire — real fire, burning down the house kind of fire.

The indoor cricket centre came five years later, in 1985. Indoor cricket was relatively new then, and the business was initially affiliated with the ICA (Indoor Cricket Association). However, the ICA demanded hefty joining fees, which my dad and his business partner, Greg Gavin, were unwilling to pay. So, they took matters into their own hands and created their own ruling body, which gave birth to the Indoor Cricket Federation (ICF).

I find the origin story here fascinating. To establish the ICF (splitting from the ICA), my dad, mum, their partners and my lifelong friends Greg and Shirley Gavin had to rewrite the rules for indoor cricket completely, ensuring they were not perceived as merely copying the ICA. They introduced innovations like eight-ball overs (compared to ICA's six-ball overs) and larger courts, ultimately reshaping the sport.

My mum spent night after night on a typewriter, rewriting indoor cricket rules, changing them enough to become their version of the sport. Over time, the ICF surpassed the ICA as the premier federation for indoor cricket. Over the decades following, my mum's rules would play out in world cups in seven countries, connecting people and families, and promoting movement and health across the world. People are still competing, winning and losing, all based on the little rule book my mum penned from her home in the mid-1980s. She didn't write it for fame or recognition, and I do not doubt that until I wrote this, very few people knew she even did that. I didn't even know; I found out through friends and family while researching this book.

Growing up in an indoor cricket centre was a unique experience. Every brick, the logo, the brand, the courts and the people were theirs. Greg, Shirley, Mum and Dad built the lot. They created a wildly successful venture in the 1980s and sold the business in the early 2000s. Eventually, around 2010, the ICF would merge into Cricket Australia, the governing body for all cricket in Australia.

The rule book that my mum handed me that day was no ordinary rule book. To Mum, it was a journal — a book of stories and memories and lessons on life. Sure, it was an ICF rule book, but it was also a testament to their involvement in the creation of the federation, from the early days back in the 1980s and through its evolution over time.

Within the weathered pages of that book, my mum had carefully preserved my childhood notes and creations. Among the pages, I discovered old poems and amusing teenage scribbles about my grand plans to break the rules. Pictures of fish and monsters, strange things I had written and lots of wisdom from Mum. I read them to her as she rested. Poems like 'The Man From Snowy River' and a few I had written, aged between about 10 and 12, folded into the pages of the rule book. Their inclusion made no sense. But they made perfect sense to Mum.

## INSIGHTS

Breaking the rules, whether through a misstep in a revered jazz club or the accidental creation of a lifelong family joke via a recorded song, often leads to unexpected avenues of innovation. Though initially a source of humour, my brother's unforgettable dance moves also stayed with me, challenging my perceptions of rhythm and self-expression. The song I recorded, intended to be a serious effort at stardom, provided my family with endless laughter and a story retold at gatherings, reinforcing the joy in life's unplanned moments.

Breaking the rules — within ethical and legal boundaries — opens our creative horizons. In creative endeavours, the intention is just the starting point; the real magic happens in the execution and the unforeseen consequences. Whether it's my mother unintentionally laying the groundwork for the growth of indoor cricket or a failed project morphing into a successful venture, these stories underscore the importance of environments that foster creativity and experimentation.

In practical terms, creating an environment conducive to creativity means removing barriers to creation and enhancing the likelihood of serendipitous innovation. If your workspace is metaphorically missing a piece that only a creative idea can fill, you're more likely to find that missing piece if the path to creation is clear and accessible. This could mean booking a recording studio without a straightforward song in mind, leaving the laptop open on a blank document, scheduling a blog post without a topic, or making sure the whiteboard is visible and inviting.

Blank pages and open spaces beg to be filled, and by ensuring these canvases are part of your daily environment, you invite the possibility of unexpected brilliance. By reducing the steps to start creating and increasing the expectation that creation will occur, you set the stage for ideas to flow more freely. This readiness to capture and develop new ideas is crucial, because it transforms passive spaces into active crucibles of creativity.

Our early experiences, the spaces we inhabit and our readiness to break the mould all shape our creative paths and career trajectories, emphasising that, sometimes, the most impactful creations arise from unexpected sources.

Our industrial systems have been designed to value predictability, which enhances efficiency and comfort. Predictability allows for a smoother supply chain and streamlined operations, making today a slightly more optimised version of yesterday.

However, true innovation — be it in creativity, breakthroughs or human connection — emerges from the unpredictable. Innovation thrives on the chaotic mingling of new ideas and perspectives, often appearing from the most unexpected quarters. Just as surprise bestsellers redefine markets, groundbreaking ideas usually burst forth from beyond the predictable scopes of our focus.

**True innovation — be it in creativity, breakthroughs or human connection — emerges from the unpredictable.**

You can bet your life that if revolutionary ideas are anticipated to come from one direction, they'll likely emerge from another. This unpredictability might be problematic, especially for those accustomed to the structured, orderly paradigms of industrial thinking. Yet, within this chaos, the most significant potential for innovation lies.

Engage with this chaos intentionally. Create environments—at work and at home—where unpredictability is tolerated and encouraged, where diverse ideas and voices can interact freely. Such conditions are fertile ground for the unexpected connections and breakthroughs that drive genuine progress.

Embracing this mindset means stepping beyond the comfort of the known and predictable, and venturing into the realm of possibility and transformation. In these dynamic interactions, the future is shaped—not just incrementally improved but fundamentally redefined.

## INSIGHTS

Don't chase perfection—focus on progress. See failure as feedback, not defeat. Stumbles and missteps are how you discover unexpected opportunities and create something new.

Remember—the true strength of creativity lies in letting failure propel you forward.

PART IV

# REFLECTIONS: MEANING

**Where you step back, reflect and ensure that your creativity is aligned with deeper values and long-term impact**

Every creative journey brings a moment when you pause and ask, 'Is this truly making a difference?' I've realised that creativity isn't just about creating — it's about creating with purpose. Taking time to reflect ensures that your work aligns with your values and the impact you wish to make. This is where confidence deepens, through knowing that your work isn't just good — it's also meaningful.

# CHAPTER 10

# THE $40000 QUESTION!

Reflecting on whether your creative efforts align
with your values

In a dimly lit boardroom, tucked away in a corner of Caboolture, north
of Brisbane, a woman sat facing the wall, her fingers dancing over a
typewriter. The setting was so odd to me and super archaic; we were
in a men's only business club, redolent of a 1930s men's club where
business was a male-only affair. The dark oak table around which
we gathered felt as much a relic as the rules that governed the club.
Oddly, in 2006, this club formed the backdrop for a pivotal meeting. It
was here that I met Mick Calder for a crucial discussion on the future
of a company caught in the throes of acquisition. Mick was a business
acquaintance who was brought in to steer the acquisition of the Oakley
business by Luxottica. I was on the steering committee, working with
Mick on integrating Oakley into the Luxottica business.

Mick, a towering figure at 6 foot 5 inches with a deep voice, loved
the ocean. As I arrived, he greeted me with a mix of jest and sincerity,
telling me he half-wished I had skipped our meeting. As he flew in,
he'd seen the surf on the nearby Sunshine Coast and thought that if
I did not show, he would have an excuse to hit the water. But business
awaited — although Mick leant in with a quick suggestion: if we could
expedite our agenda, we could still catch some waves before flying
back to Sydney. This proposal marked the beginning of an enduring,
lifelong friendship.

As we settled in, the presence of the woman relegated to the margins of the room, her role confined to recording minutes on a typewriter facing the wall, underscored the dated practices still at play. It was a stark reminder of the slow pace of change within some corporate sectors in Australia. Mick, perhaps sensing my discomfort with the arrangement (along with me lipping the words 'What the actual fuck is she doing in the corner?'), broke the tradition. He invited the woman to join us at the table, a clear and sensible inclusion that spoke volumes about his leadership style. He made her a cup of coffee gave her a respectful nod, and then went further. He not only brought her into the circle (I assume a first for the men's club) but also set a new tone — 'You can leave the typewriter in the corner, and I can take notes', he stated. This wasn't just about challenging tradition — it was about leadership, about creating space for others.

That's the thing about creativity. It's not just about coming up with clever ideas. It's also about shifting perspectives, challenging the status quo and making space for new voices. Creativity, in its essence, is deeply connected to leadership. Mick wasn't just steering a billion-dollar acquisition; he was setting the tone for how business could be done differently, and more inclusively.

Mick's business acumen, which allowed for a smooth navigation of the Oakley acquisition, was widely recognised. As we discussed strategies and outcomes, his approach was innovative and inclusive. His insights into the shifting dynamics of business were not just theoretical; they were also backed by actionable experience and a clear vision for the future. Today, he remains one of the most intelligent business leaders (at the big end-of-town kind of business) I have ever met. I can sit for hours listening to Mick's stories of billion-dollar mergers.

The meeting in Caboolture was brief yet impactful, with Mick steering discussions with the ease of a seasoned captain.

At the same time, my three years at Luxottica were drawing to a close. I had always told myself to give the role three years, allowing me to settle in and see what I could do. But now, after three years, the paths before me were sharply defined: one led to the role of CEO at Oakley, a job I wanted to explore, to continue my corporate journey; the other, a leap into the unknown, to establish my consultancy focused on solving complex problems. This choice was more than a career decision; it reflected my personal and professional evolution.

# INSIGHTS

I have always admired Luxottica. I still do; indeed, I am forever in awe of anything that employs people—and Luxottica has employed over 100 000 humans. In my haze of not knowing how to scale a business, I am forever drawn to the people who can. One of those great business minds along the journey was Leonardo Del Vecchio, the founder of Luxottica.

Leonardo's life is a tale of overcoming adversity. His parents, emigrants from Puglia in the south of Italy, sought a better life in the north of the country. However, Leonardo's father, a produce vendor, passed away before he was born (in 1935). Amid the turmoil of World War II, his mother then faced the heart-wrenching decision to place seven-year-old Leonardo in an orphanage. It was a defining moment in his early life that would shape his future. Leonardo's journey from those challenging beginnings to the helm of Luxottica is a testament to his resilience and vision.

Leonardo's foray into the business world began at the tender age of 14. His subsequent journey, marked by ambition and resilience, saw a pivotal turn when, at 25, he established his first factory under the Luxottica brand. This venture took root in Agordo, a town cradled in the Dolomites of north-eastern Italy, known for its scenic beauty as much as its dynamic spirit. Leonardo secured the land for his factory at no cost, a move facilitated by a local initiative to stimulate the economy. This deal was struck on the promise of job creation for the area, and was a testament to Leonardo's entrepreneurial acumen and unwavering determination.

Under Leonardo's leadership, Luxottica transformed into an eyewear empire. Its expansion strategy included taking control of recognised brands such as Ray-Ban and Oakley, cementing its status as a titan along the way. But perhaps more notably, Leonardo was a visionary in brand licensing—a strategy that propelled Luxottica to new heights in the 1980s.

Leonardo's foresight led to licensing agreements with the crème de la crème of the fashion world. Luxottica bridged the gap between high fashion and eyewear by collaborating with illustrious labels such as Dolce & Gabbana, Versace and Chanel. These partnerships allowed the company to craft collections that mirrored the elegance and prestige of these luxury brands, further expanding Luxottica's reach and impact in the fashion eyewear sector.

*(continued)*

His keen eye for the potential in licensing and strategic partnerships with luxury fashion houses was pivotal in Luxottica's ascent. Leonardo's influence in the eyewear industry wasn't just confined to manufacturing, however; it was about fusing fashion with functionality, understanding the market's pulse, and responding with innovation and style.

Upon Leonardo's passing in 2022, Forbes acknowledged him as one of the world's wealthiest individuals, with an estimated net worth of $27.3 billion. Yet, despite his colossal success and financial acumen, he remained grounded, often seen as a humble figure against the backdrop of Italy's striking business and political elite.

Leonardo Del Vecchio and his impact on a narrow sector within fashion fascinated me. During my time at Luxottica, Milan, one of my favourite cities, became a second home of sorts. Every three months, I would board a plane, land at the same airport, and the same driver would greet me and whisk me away to the same hotel. My routine was almost ritualistic: suits pressed by attentive room service staff, meetings conducted in Italian, and feeling a part of something grand. I was in Leonardo's world now.

My work would lead me to attend trade shows such as Silmo in Paris, ODMA in Sydney, Bread & Butter in Berlin, Pitti Uomo in Florence, and Action Sports Retailer in San Diego and Los Angeles. But Milan was a regular stop, and (as I've mentioned in previous chapters) a long way from the streets of Penrith where I grew up.

The visits to Milan and the events I attended were not just about business; they were also about forging connections, building relationships, and immersing myself in the vibrant world of eyewear and fashion. I would often bring essential buyers from prominent Australian retailers such as Myer or David Jones to these trade shows, introducing them to the industry's intricacies.

On my trips with Luxottica, at the end of my three-day journey from Milan via Venice, often with clients in tow, I would rent a car and drive into the mountains to Agordo, the home of Luxottica and Leonardo Del Vecchio's hometown. I was fond of this place, and the scenic drive from Venice into the Dolomites remains fresh in my memory. I can recall every turn. My time in Agordo went beyond business; it was an opportunity to immerse myself in the place's rich history and culture.

Agordo was a testament to Leonardo's commitment to his community. At the time, the town was home to main Luxottica factory and headquarters — and these were monumental, both in scale and significance. It was here that the industry giant began his journey as an independent machinist, supplying eyewear parts to other regional manufacturers. Over time, Leonardo had turned the headquarters into a breeding ground for a world of innovation — metal eyewear parts being plated, polishing tumblers whirring with precision, giant CAD-design computer stations, and an enormous cafeteria bustling with activity. Corporate offices buzzed with energy, and a sprawling parking lot seemed to blend with what appeared to be mix a ski chalet, hunting lodge and home right in its midst. I found out Leonardo's house sat smack bang in the middle, untouched by development; it was almost perfect. I learned he employed most of the town's residents and had also acquired local vineyards and farms. The produce from these lands would nourish his staff and, as his business grew, he even provided free transportation to Agordo, along with complimentary food and wine for his employees. His dedication to his people left a mark on me.

During my time at Luxottica, I had a few mini-encounters with Leonardo directly. One morning, our paths crossed in the unlikeliest place — the staff cafeteria at the Luxottica office in Agordo. He spoke in Italian, a language I partially understood, and his presence was magnetic. Meeting him felt akin to meeting a music icon, similar to coming face to face with Bono. I was not just in the company of a man; the history he created surrounded me.

I couldn't resist capturing the essence of this place through my camera lens. I snapped photos of the facility, and once grabbed some candid moments of Leonardo and his family enjoying lunch with the staff in the Luxottica cafe. But the real magic happened at the end of the workday.

As Luxottica's employees poured out of the facility, they formed a jubilant crowd heading toward lines of corporate buses that would take them home to the picturesque Cadore mountainside towns. It was a scene reminiscent of fans leaving a stadium after a victorious game, an atmosphere of fulfilled satisfaction.

Amid this sea of smiles and contentment, my gaze once shifted towards the parking lot. Leonardo stood on a distinctive house balcony, watching over his Luxottica 'family' as they departed for the night.

I witnessed not just the head of a global eyewear empire but also a leader who cared deeply about his team. It was a snapshot of genuine

> **Our journeys can intersect with the stories of remarkable individuals, creating lasting admiration and a sense of awe of the legacy they've created.**

connection and shared purpose, and a testament to the leader Leonardo was — one who led with his heart and vision.

Leonardo Del Vecchio's story, from his humble beginnings to becoming the visionary founder of Luxottica, was an inspiration to me. His impact on the eyewear industry and the communities he touched was profound. As I reflect on those moments, I'm reminded that our journeys can intersect with the stories of remarkable individuals, creating lasting admiration and a sense of awe of the legacy they've created. I was and will always remain in awe of Leonardo.

## INSIGHTS

My time at Luxottica was transformative, guided by remarkable mentors such as Rhonda Brighton-Hall. Rhonda, a former CEO at Sara Lee and a Telstra Businesswoman of the Year, now leads mwah (making work absolutely human). Her insights and guidance during my Luxottica days helped shape my approach to life and work.

One enduring lesson from Rhonda was the 'power of five'. She encouraged us to make five decisions and take five actions each day. She based this on the belief that if a task couldn't fit into the palm of our hand, we were much more likely to deem it too overwhelming. This simple yet profound principle still guides my daily choices.

Rhonda's teachings extended beyond decision-making, delving into genuine change and exploring the intricacies of human behaviour. I hung on her every word and remain captivated by her wisdom.

My three years at Luxottica, collaborating with Rhonda and her exceptional team, especially Chip Liedel, were transformative. During this period, I immersed myself in the world of process-improvement tool Six Sigma and ignited an insatiable passion for creativity.

In those years, as I've mentioned, I collaborated with iconic brands such as Dolce & Gabbana, Chanel, Prada, Versace and Miu Miu. Sitting in brand meetings and strategy sessions with leaders from these revered fashion houses forever shaped my understanding of brand identity, luxury and why people invest in these communities.

I delved deep into consumers' psyches, unravelling the subtle distinctions between 'Made in Italy' and 'Made in China'. My fascination with production, quality and the artistry of craftsmanship led me to appreciate making things. Witnessing the precision of Luxottica's manufacturing process left me yearning for the personal touch of handmade craftsmanship.

My Luxottica journey was more than a professional experience; it was also a profound exploration of creativity, human behaviour and the luxury journey. This time in my life fuelled my lifelong passion for craftsmanship and authenticity.

Luxottica was a vast company boasting an extensive advisory team and a formidable senior management team. Rhonda's unparalleled charisma and ability to take charge infused the business with radiant energy. Her leadership wasn't just about deciding and moving things forward with undeniable positive momentum. She was a catalyst for change and an inspirational force that ignited organisational transformation.

## INSIGHTS

Chip Liedel, another mentor and lifelong connection formed during my time at Luxottica, also taught me about leadership and human connection. With over 30 years of experience in leadership, coaching and management development, he forever altered my worldview. Born in Detroit, Chip navigated a world of complexity and change, moving through cities such as New York and Sydney, and inspiring people wherever he went.

One of Chip's most profound qualities is his ability to lead with emotional intelligence (EQ). He taught me that while cognitive intelligence (IQ) is essential, EQ sets exceptional leaders apart. His empathy, self-awareness and social awareness expertise have shaped my understanding of effective leadership.

*(continued)*

Rhonda and Chip showed that leadership isn't just about making calculated decisions based on data; it's also about connecting with people on a profoundly emotional level, understanding their motivations and inspiring them to reach their fullest potential.

This lesson on emotional intelligence transcended the boundaries of the corporate world and became a guiding principle in my leadership journey. It taught me that the essence of authentic leadership is the ability to empathise, connect and uplift others. I carry this lesson with me in every facet of my life, reminding me that the human element is at the heart of all meaningful endeavours.

During my time at Luxottica, I learned from inspirational leaders about who I wanted to become and, more importantly, what kind of leader I didn't want to be.

As I mention earlier in this chapter, when I first joined Luxottica, I gave myself a three-year timeline. While I missed the entrepreneurial spirit of my previous undertakings, I was intrigued by the corporate world. I was hungry to learn, to immerse myself and to entertain the idea that this could become my future path.

As time went by, however, I found that the more I invested in my role, the further I drifted away from the realm of creativity. Senior management meetings served as stark reminders that profit came first, sometimes at any cost. I came to understand that as a brand manufacturer and retailer, the margins reaped through our retail doors far surpassed any other considerations.

In this pursuit of growth and profit, I witnessed the harsh reality of third-party squeezing — that is, small businesses being squeezed out of the high street to make room for more 'owned' stores. I saw Sunglass Hut outlets spring up next door to eyewear stores selling the same brands Luxottica supplied. Sunglass Hut compelled the family-owned stores to shut their doors by selling these brands at significant discounts for months, making way for Luxottica's expansion. I was part of those meetings, witnessing the unrelenting drive for growth at all costs. For a while, it was intoxicating, and I drank the corporate Kool-Aid, yearning to understand more.

In this complex landscape, I also witnessed a dichotomy of leadership styles. On the one hand, the leadership team demanded results at any cost, prioritising a relentless pursuit of numbers. Rhonda and the HR team, on the other hand, advocated for connection, personalisation and genuine care for the people behind the business. But the yearning for connection stopped at the door. We didn't care about people outside the tent; we cared about our people because our people were the tools for growth.

The lessons I absorbed during those three years at Luxottica were not just about profit and growth, but also about understanding the leader I aspired to be. I found inspiration in the passionate individuals within the company, but the singular focus on numbers equally deflated me. My journey at Luxottica became a crucible for learning, shaping my perspective on leadership, ethics and the human element within business.

My three years at Luxottica drew almost to an end, and change was on the horizon. After the company's acquisition of Oakley Eyewear (for a hefty sum), I found myself stretched across the steering committee, navigating this intriguing phase of my business life.

The pivotal moment in my Luxottica journey came during a dinner conversation with Nicola, as we delved into the concept of purpose. We discussed finding that one thing I was good at. Rhonda had played a significant role in helping me discover it, but I wasn't living it in my current job. My head advised me to stay, considering the attractive salary, rewarding work and job security. But my heart was telling me to go, to create something meaningful.

The opportunity to become the CEO of Oakley seemed the perfect fit, balancing both my head and my heart. Oakley was still a medium-sized company, operating in industries I loved — snowboarding, snow sports, surfing and skating. I decided I wanted this role. After a rigorous interview, I was deemed the right person for the job, and the existing CEO, Paul Higgins, also a good friend, gave me the green light.

However, my Luxottica CEO had other plans. He needed me to remain in my current position. Luxottica had its strategic agenda, and moving to Oakley was no longer an option. The opportunity I had longed for had vanished.

Left with only one option, I followed in Mick Calder's footsteps and created my dream job for myself. Before my departure, however, Nicola advised me to discuss my feelings with the existing Luxottica CEO. So, I did just that. I expressed my conflicting feelings and spoke openly, sharing that my heart was yearning to venture out and create, while my head was inclined to stay. I asked him to convince me to stay, to give me a compelling reason to remain. I expressed my desire to tackle challenges, to find my purpose and to do exceptional work.

We met at 7 am on a Monday, because he had a flight to South Africa at 11 am. After sharing my aspirations, laying my heart on the line, he slid a napkin across the table. On it was written, '$40 000'. With a smile, he asked, 'Now, what does your heart tell you?'

I thanked him for his time and registered my company 6.2 the next day.

It was a moment of reckoning, a crossroads where the path of least resistance diverged from the road less travelled. I picked the latter and, in doing so, I picked myself.

Our lives will deliver us lessons and limitations. From the incredible Leonardo Del Vecchio to the transformative influence of Rhonda Brighton-Hall and Chip Liedel and the leadership of Mick Calder and Paul Higgins, I encountered a certain person who became a chapter in my story. The same is true for your story Each person you meet adds depth and dimension to your understanding of what it means to lead (and be led).

> **The most compelling narratives are those that remain unwritten — the stories you are yet to live, the adventures you're yet to embark on, and the lives you're yet to touch.**

The most compelling narratives are those that remain unwritten — the stories you are yet to live, the adventures you're yet to embark on, and the lives you're yet to touch. Ultimately, the most extraordinary journeys bring you closer to understanding who you are and who you aspire to be.

And that is worth more than $40 000.

## INSIGHTS

Real impact happens when you choose authenticity over comfort, even when it's tough. Your biggest growth often comes from taking the harder path — the one that aligns with your values, not just your goals.

When faced with a decision, ask yourself: 'Am I staying true to my purpose, or am I settling for what's easy?' The most meaningful journeys aren't always the easiest, but they're the ones that bring you closer to your true self.

Choose authenticity, even when it comes at a cost.

CHAPTER 11

# A REAL-LIFE SUPER SUIT

Considering the real-world impact of your
creative choices

The ocean has always been my refuge, a place where I can escape
the relentless buzz of technology. There are no pings, texts or
vibrations — just me and the expanse of nature. It's where I find peace
and recharge, a setting almost meditative in its simplicity. After an
early surf session one morning, I still found myself caught in a moment
of procrastination, searching for the motivation to kick-start my day.
I stumbled on the following quote from science fiction author and
screenwriter Ray Bradbury:

> Don't think. Thinking is the enemy of creativity. It's self-conscious,
> and anything self-conscious is lousy. You can't try to do things.
> You simply must do things.

This is now a quote I often return to.

In the mid-2000s, I shared an office with former pro surfer Kye
Fitzgerald and his brother Joel. We spent about five years together,
building a lifetime bond. Their dad owned Hot Buttered Surfboards
and, around that time, Kye was also making waves with his surf label,
18 People. It was a period of unfiltered creativity for me, driven by
instinct and a shared passion for surf culture.

During this time, I needed a new surfboard, and we struck a deal. Kye had some old stock going cheap — authentic cheap — and I was hooked. As a small business owner, I always looked for savings, and surfboards were expensive. I headed to the Hot Buttered head office, in Warriewood in northern Sydney, to pick them up.

When I arrived, I faced a quirky dilemma: the two boards set aside for me, for the super low price, were in striking colours — awkwardly striking. The kind of colours you can see before you actually see them, glowing like the bright light emanating from the briefcase in *Pulp Fiction*. One was a bright purple and the other was a vivid mix of yellow and orange. As I approached, they almost hurt my eyes. Kye had mentioned they were the unsellable stock, so I knew they weren't your everyday boards, but I had envisaged nothing so bright. The size and specs were spot on, however. In fulfilling our deal, I ended up with these eye-catching boards. I gave my friend Webby the 6-foot-3-inch yellow board and took the 6-foot-4-inch' purple one for myself.

I didn't really mind; all I needed was a board to surf, regardless of its colour. Or so I thought. It didn't take long for the jokes to start. At my local beach, I became known as 'Grimace', while Webby earned the nickname 'Ronald McDonald' at his break. It took 24 hours for these names to stick and then there I was, forever dubbed Grimace. Even when I switched to my sleek, white McTavish, the Grimace jokes followed.

On a surf trip to Byron Bay, I was alone in the water, enjoying a little wave far from the crowds, with Grimace in tow. I noticed a guy about 500 metres away, waving at me. As he paddled closer, I realised I didn't know him. He introduced himself as Mark and asked where I got my purple board. After I explained the deal with Hot Buttered, he burst out laughing and slapped the water, overwhelmed by emotion. 'What's up?' I asked, to which he confessed that he'd made a bet years ago with Kye and Terry Fitzgerald that they'd never sell a fluoro purple board. I was the sucker who proved him wrong and cost Mark $100.

Eventually, I passed the board on to a friend in Stanwell Park, where it continued to turn heads and live its bright life.

## INSIGHTS

I often retell this tale about my bright purple surfboard. It delves into the intricate balance of our choices and their silent declarations about our identity. It also underscores the ties we forge with brands, and the emotional resonance stirred by a product and what these products represent — what they say about us. This isn't about the superficial allure of a brand; it's about what that brand mirrors — the culture it embodies and the niche it carves in society.

Nike's iconic swoosh — a simple curve and a sharp point — speaks volumes. It's not just the elegance of the design that captivates us; it's the trust and familiarity we've nurtured with the brand over countless years. That swoosh isn't a logo; it's a repository of our shared history, a symbol of the athletic feats and aspirations it represents. As Sallie Krawcheck, CEO and co-founder of Ellevest and a prominent advocate for women leaders in business, once said, 'We build trust in tiny moments'.

Reflecting on my Grimace surfboard story, I realise it was not so much a board but a statement. That purple board wasn't just a piece of equipment; it was also a declaration of my identity, much like how a brand's logo speaks volumes about its ethos and culture. Just as that surfboard spoke to the surfers about me, the Nike logo triggers a sentiment that connects us to a legacy of athletic excellence.

Imagine a spectrum, a line stretching from left to right. On one end lies the market's perception of your brand and business, and, on the other, is your narrative about yourself. The proper task is to find that sweet spot in the middle, where what you say about yourself aligns with how the world sees you. Sadly, this is where many brands falter. As Whitney Wolfe Herd, founder of Bumble, noted, 'We must redefine success in our terms'. Many brands struggle to align their internal narratives with external perceptions, creating a discord between self-perception and public image.

The challenge lies in realigning perceptions, which demands clarity, integrity and a commitment to your values. Life is much the same. And while I don't recommend obsessing over what people think of you, ensuring that your values on one end of the spectrum align with your relationships on the other is crucial. Do you have strong relationships because what you say reflects what people see in you? Are you creating genuine connections and actual bonds? As Indra Nooyi, former CEO of PepsiCo, said, 'The distance between number one and number two is always constant. If you want to improve the organisation, you must improve yourself'. This holds in business and life — aligning your internal values with your external relationships is critical to genuine connection and success.

> **In an ever-watchful world, the congruence between what we project and what we indeed are is the cornerstone of trust and respect.**

Every day, we put the authenticity of our message to the test. Any mismatch is immediately apparent. Just as a brand that can't hide from broken trust, our brand cannot mask the misalignment between our values and people's perceptions. If we are not authentic, honest and transparent, we are found out, one way or another. People will know and this should serve as potent reminder of the power of authenticity. It's a call to action for brands and individuals to align their internal narrative with their external image — who they are and how they wish to be perceived. In an ever-watchful world, the congruence between what we project and what we indeed are is the cornerstone of trust and respect.

Arianna Huffington said, 'We need to accept that we won't always make the right decisions, but we have to be committed to the values that guide those decisions.' I love this; it underscores the importance of authenticity in both personal and professional realms.

Robert Sternberg, a psychologist renowned for his multi-decade research on facets such as intelligence, wisdom and leadership, found a common thread among all the creative individuals he studied. At a pivotal moment, they choose to be creative. This choice manifests in several ways:

- Creative individuals redefine problems through unique lenses, opening up novel avenues for solutions.
- They embrace sensible risks and view failure as essential to the innovation journey.
- They courageously confront and navigate the inevitable roadblocks that arise when questioning established norms.
- They willingly endure uncertainty, allowing them to navigate ambiguous terrains without assuring success.
- They resist intellectual stagnation, evolving their skills and knowledge.

Sternberg argues that fostering creativity in psychological contexts would be more successful if the emphasis were placed on making this crucial decision to be creative, celebrating the joys it brings and preparing individuals for the accompanying challenges. Creativity isn't a passive trait; it's an active choice and seldom does it align with the path of least resistance.

In my two decades immersed in innovative design, I've encountered a prevailing belief that creativity is an inherent trait akin to eye colour — you've either got it or you don't. This notion is a myth. Creativity is not some rare gift given to a select few; it is a universal attribute in everyone.

It's high time we challenge this myth and foster a broader understanding of creativity. Now more than ever, the world needs individuals to recognise and believe in their creative potential. This is why I'm so focused on creative confidence, which captures this belief that creativity isn't the exclusive domain of 'creatives' but a natural attribute in all of us. This confidence empowers us to harness our innate creativity and apply it to various aspects of our lives and work, regardless of the field or discipline.

Think about it — every problem we encounter, every challenge we face, provides a canvas for our creativity. Creativity isn't reserved for the arts or design; it's about innovating ways to communicate, solve problems, lead and think. Creative confidence invites us to view challenges as opportunities to inject creativity into, experimenting, exploring and transforming the mundane into something extraordinary.

Encouraging this mindset is about personal growth *and* societal evolution. When people embrace their creative potential, they become proactive community contributors. They drive change, inspire innovation, and see possibilities where others see obstacles.

◊◊◊

When Jake Burton Carpenter entered the winter sports scene in 1977 as a snowboarder, he faced a landscape rife with scepticism. People dismissed snowboarding as a fleeting fad, an eccentric offshoot of skiing — a joke. But Jake saw beyond the doubters. To him, the slopes were a canvas of untapped potential, a new way to connect with the world. He wasn't so much creating a product as reshaping how we think about winter sports. In those early days, Jake said, 'The sport had kicked off in the late 1970s, but it was illegal in mountain resorts, and I was part of the crusade to change that'.

My journey into snowboarding began at 16, working at Off the Edge, a snowboard shop in Penrith. I was attracted to the job because of my early love for snow sports, which was nurtured by the weekend ski trips with my dad I talk about in chapter 3. I got my job at Off the Edge the old-fashioned way — at 15, I walked in and dropped off my resume, typed on a piece of paper from a typewriter. The owners, Briggette and Keith, grilled me with a thousand questions about Australian snow resorts and my connection to the alpine. When they confirmed my passion matched theirs, I got the job, working Thursday nights and Sunday mornings. My bond with Briggette and Keith remains strong, and their support allowed me to break in the latest demo gear on our ski trips.

My first day of snowboarding was with Briggette's son, Ben, at Perisher in 1991. I remember the wild exhilaration of that day, strapped into a 1991 Burton Air Craig Kelly pro model. The board, a vivid directional piece, was a testament to Jake Burton's dedication to supporting athletes in snow sports. I wore Sorel hiking boots in the early days, which I later traded for a pair of Northwave. Still, the feeling of freedom on that first descent was unforgettable — I felt like I was at the start of a revolution.

Snowboarding in Australia gained traction in the late 1980s and early 1990s, with resorts such as Perisher and Thredbo becoming popular among enthusiasts. Jake's vision extended far beyond his Vermont barn. It moved into public forums, events and narratives, weaving a vibrant community and culture around snowboarding. He distilled his ethos into a simple yet powerful mantra: 'If it's not fun, why do it? We're driven by a simple formula: innovation + people'. With each snowboard he crafted, every event he sponsored and every story he shared, Jake was building trust and adding value to a realm that had long dismissed his sport.

## INSIGHTS

Jake Burton Carpenter was a pioneering figure in high-performance snow sports and was crucial in integrating snowboarding into the broader sporting world. He championed the sport's entry into the Olympics, starting with the Nagano Winter Games in 1998. Under the guidance of him and his wife, Donna, Burton Snowboards grew into a $200 million business that became a living embodiment of winter sports culture for generations.

Jake understood branding early on, knowing how to connect the dots between design, brand, product and culture. Despite initial perceptions of snowboarding as an 'alternative sport', Jake's unwavering support helped propel it into mainstream recognition.

Jake met Donna at a bar on New Year's Eve in 1981, and the couple spent their 35-year marriage collaborating at Burton. Donna worked in production, dipping snowboards in polyurethane, and managing customer service, helping to expand the company before taking on the CEO role in 2015. Today, Donna has transformed the company into a B Corp (demonstrating high social and environmental performance) and a beacon of social and climate impact as the brand strives for inclusive and impactful climate initiatives.

The brand has supported hundreds of athletes, including Shaun White, Chloe Kim and Kelly Clark, fostering a new generation of snowboarding talent. Jake's influence also extended beyond snowboarding, however. He collaborated with notable celebrities and artists such as Jeff Koons and Gwen Stefani, who found the brand's ethos appealing. His approach to business was not just about profit, but also about building a community and embedding his operations within a social responsibility framework, leading Burton to become a certified B Corp.

Jake's life was a masterclass in reimagining the world. He didn't just observe what was around him; he envisioned what could be and pursued it relentlessly. His legacy in snowboarding and beyond is a testament to the power of creativity, resilience and the courage to challenge the status quo.

Jake faced many health battles, from testicular cancer to a rare nerve disease called Miller Fisher syndrome, which left him temporarily paralysed. During these health challenges, in 2018 he launched Mine77, a personal second line of apparel and gear, reflecting his resilience and creativity. Each item in the Mine77 collection was crafted with a personal touch, tailored to Jake's specific needs and experiences, from compression socks to the innovative Over Helmet, designed to prevent severe head injuries.

Jake passed away in 2019 at 65 because of complications from cancer, leaving behind a legacy as the godfather of snowboarding, and a visionary who turned a fringe sport into a global phenomenon.

How do you plot your course in the world? How do you build the thing you can't stop thinking about? You need to have the destination in mind *and* understand the why behind wanting to get there. This is where a good problem statement comes in — transforming it from a project tool into a powerful life tool.

**You need to have the destination in mind *and* understand the why behind wanting to get there.**

Creating a problem statement is an art form in itself, and goes far beyond ticking off an item on your to-do list. The good news is, however, it's not as complicated as it might seem. The key is understanding the how. You need to unleash your inner wellspring of resourcefulness, tapping into your innate, childlike ability to create, problem-solve and learn continuously. Within these skills lies the subtle art of defining a critical question — a question with an answer that has the potential to transform everything.

Think about game-changers like Burton Snowboards; they didn't just follow the trends — they turned an entire industry on its head. This kind of seismic shift begins with identifying that pivotal question. It's that 'big bang' moment that sparks all subsequent innovation. It's about finding that one question that, once answered, illuminates the path forward and ignites a chain reaction of creativity and discovery.

Jake Burton Carpenter's journey is a testament to this approach. He didn't just ask, 'How do I build a snowboard?' He asked, 'How do I make snowboarding accessible to everyone?' That kind of question transforms industries and inspires movements. The focus is no longer on the product but the experience, culture and community surrounding it. That's the power of a well-defined problem statement — the seed from which revolutionary ideas grow.

I asked the simple question: 'What can design do?' This seems straightforward, but it's nuanced. To me, design has the power to change the world. Consider the figure I mention in chapter 7: 80 per cent of the environmental impact of a product originate in the design phase. So, 'What can design do?' Framing the question in this way highlights design is not just about aesthetics or functionality; it's also about envisioning and shaping a sustainable future. It's about creating solutions that are not only innovative but also responsible. Design is where the blueprint for impact is laid out. It's where we decide whether a product will contribute to the problem or be part of the solution.

When Jake asked how to make snowboarding accessible to everyone, he wasn't just designing a snowboard but a movement. By asking 'What can design do?' we open the door to transformative possibilities. We challenge ourselves to think beyond the conventional and to create with purpose. We start embedding sustainability into the very fabric of our creative processes.

The 'creative' roles have been confined to their corner for far too long, isolated from the 'serious' aspects of business. While at Luxottica, I often questioned why the boardroom, too often dominated by white men in suits with functional backgrounds, approached problem-solving in ways disconnected from empathy and vulnerability. These people rarely stepped into the customer's shoes; instead, their references were spreadsheets, numbers and budgets. While they built a multibillion-dollar company and did many things right, they also did wrong things that mattered to their people!

Many talented individuals I knew left, feeling something was off. What if they had stayed? What if someone had given them the power to break free from their designated niches? That's the lingering question — what if?!

## INSIGHTS

Times have changed. Creativity is no longer just a decorative ornament and is now the engine of innovation. Education leaders such as Sir Ken Robinson argued that creativity is as critical to education as literacy. Creativity has transcended its artistic boundaries in today's business landscape to become synonymous with innovation. Tech giants such as Google and Facebook have changed our lives by letting their employees' creativity flourish without constraint. This force has permeated every facet of business, proving that innovative insights can come from any corner of an organisation. A recent IBM Global CEO survey found that creativity is our complex global economy's most vital leadership quality. Yet, according to an Adobe Systems State of Create poll, only 25 per cent of people believe they are reaching their creative potential. That's a lot of untapped talent.

So, how do we ignite the dormant creativity in the remaining 75 per cent of people? At Reny, our workshops and collaborations with clients have shown that reigniting imagination, curiosity and courage takes only the smallest of nudges. The impact on the executives we've worked with is immediate, liberating and transformative. The realisation that they are far more creative than they thought often surprises them, and the thrill of that first breakthrough spurs them on with creative confidence.

We don't have to invent creativity; it's already within us. The challenge is nurturing it and fostering an environment where ideas can emerge and be acted upon. This blend of creative thinking and actionable courage is crucial.

*(continued)*

Thupten Jinpa Langri, the Dalai Lama's long-time English translator, offers a refreshing perspective here: the Tibetan language doesn't have a word for 'creativity'; the closest term is 'natural'. This fits, because creativity was our natural state in childhood, when we were unburdened by fear or social stigma. Reclaiming it, even decades later, is possible and liberating.

Unblocking creativity can lead to monumental shifts in our lives, organisations and communities. If you can harness this innate resource, the possibilities are limitless. Your collective creative energy is your most untapped and valuable asset, and a catalyst for solving complex challenges today.

It's staggering to think that our educational systems, designed for a bygone era, too often hinder the full expression of human creativity. The questions focused on in schools are wrong — they are upside down. We shouldn't be asking, 'How intelligent are you?' but 'How are you intelligent?' This shift in perspective changes everything.

Again, this comes back to a well-articulated problem statement and how it can create a map of your journey. Without it, you're likely to wander. The effort you invest in crafting your problem statement dictates your project's direction and can influence your long-term goals. It serves as the foundation for launching all innovative solutions.

Take your time with crafting this statement, be patient and trust yourself. You don't need to rush. Create your timeline. The workaholic hero narrative is outdated and detrimental to wellbeing. Prioritising balance is vital to meaningful, sustainable work. I'm not talking here about the balance your boss talks about — work–life balance, instigated by your company or boss, is the wrong kind. This is your life; you choose your balance.

Working all the time doesn't equate to working smart. Rather than a badge of commitment, it's one of inefficiency. The workaholic mentality creates more problems than it solves, turning minor issues into crises. It contributes to poor morale and less productive employees, creating a toxic work environment.

The antidote to overworking isn't idleness, however, it's finding equilibrium. Proper balance is a personal responsibility. Influential leaders understand that inspiration doesn't come from endless labour, but from tuning into internal rhythms and understanding cycles of creativity.

When I founded Reny, I knew my inspiration came from ski resorts, cafes and moments with my kids on the slopes. I found my creative balance in these spaces, proving that one doesn't have to be deskbound to create.

I've learned that my creativity peaks between 6 am and 11 am, and so I dedicate this time to conceptual work. After midday is for meetings, exercise and refreshments. Evenings are for family, and late nights are for deep-focus work. This balanced cadence respects both my work and wellbeing.

Reject the glorification of overwork. Find your rhythm, understand your productivity cycles and make your time count. Work should be a part of life, not the other way around. True heroes know when to hang up the cape, trusting tomorrow will bring new opportunities — maybe even for the greater good. True heroes know when to hang up their capes (or Super Suit, each to their own), trusting that tomorrow will bring new opportunities for impact.

> **Reject the glorification of overwork. Find your rhythm, understand your productivity cycles and make your time count.**

Important here also is alignment instead of agreement, because this underlines shared understanding over consensus. Agreement is compromise; alignment is unity. Creativity thrives when aligned with the problem to be solved.

Remember that the journey is shared. While you may originate with the vision, you also need to surround yourself with trusted people aligned with your vision. Together, you won't just make something happen — you will create something extraordinary.

# INSIGHTS

Trust your instincts, and don't overthink your ideas and responses. Often, the best creative breakthroughs come from simply taking action and embracing the moment, even when the path is unclear.

Stay committed to your purpose, but be ready to adjust course as needed. True creativity is about moving forward while remaining open to change.

# CHAPTER 12

# DESIGN MATTERS

Aligning your creativity with meaning and purpose

On a scorching summer day in 1980 at Maroubra Beach, Sydney, I had an encounter with a can of Mello Yello soft drink that would stick with me forever. As a kid, cracking a soft drink on a hot day felt like I was unlocking a little piece of paradise — a ritual of summer wrapped in aluminium. But the design of those cans was peculiar: you had to press a small hole first before the larger one, releasing the gas and pressure. It was a quirky mechanism that seemed almost magical to my young eyes — until it wasn't.

My excitement quickly turned into panic when my thumb got stuck in my haste to open the can. I yelped in pain as Dad tried to pry me free while Mum watched on, her scepticism of beach outings justified in an instant. From that day on, I was terrified of soda cans, forever handing them off to someone else to open. It was a minor childhood trauma, but one that sparked an obsession with the everyday objects we often overlook.

The history of the soda can is a lesson in how design evolves — and, sometimes, how it fails. Early cans had pull tabs that detached entirely, a seemingly simple solution. Strangely, however, pull tabs were dangerous, and countless injuries occurred, including lost fingers and toes, and even deaths from people accidentally ingesting the sharp tabs. That something as mundane as a soda can could be deadly is staggering. The industry responded with the Sta-Tab, a ring pull that stayed attached, reducing litter and hazards, but still not perfect. Even today's design, refined for safety and sustainability, is far from flawless.

It's a reminder that every design responds to a problem but rarely a final answer.

Everything around us was designed by someone, somewhere — beginning as a thought, a sketch, a prototype turned reality. While often touted as our great saviour, design has been complicit in many of our modern challenges. If design thinking was supposed to be the answer, why do we have so many problems caused by design? For every problem an innovation solves, it seems to create new ones, too. Plastic solved packaging, for example, until it clogged our oceans. Cars gave us freedom but chained us to fossil fuels. The soda can, now supposedly perfected, still adds billions of units to landfills each year.

'Design thinking' emerged as a movement in the 1990s and developed through the 2000s, promising a way to solve complex problems by focusing on human needs. The outlined process was empathise, define, ideate, prototype, test and implement — a structured approach to creativity that felt like a roadmap to a better world. But maybe, just maybe, design thinking is flawed, too. If a design process was truly human-centred, why did it allow for the rise of single-use plastics, devices built for obsolescence, and products that, while meeting consumer needs, quietly eroded our planet?

The term 'eco-design' was supposed to signal a shift — towards a responsible, thoughtful approach to making things that do not harm. But isn't that what good design was meant to be all along? It's frustrating that we need a term to remind us to consider the consequences of what we create. It's like needing to label yourself a 'good person'. Shouldn't that be the baseline?

## INSIGHTS

As I've mentioned a few times, an estimated 80 per cent of a product's environmental impact is determined in the design phase. That's a staggering amount of responsibility placed in the hands of designers. The choices made at the drawing board can dictate a product's entire lifecycle — from its carbon footprint to the waste it leaves behind. Design's potential is immense, but so is its capacity to harm.

We've been sold on design thinking as the cure-all, but it's time to question the efficacy of this methodology when the evidence of its flaws is all around us. The real challenge isn't perfecting the process but redefining what it means to design responsibly. We all need to ask tougher questions, hold ourselves accountable and recognise that good design is about more than aesthetics or function — it's about ensuring what we create truly makes the world better, not just easier.

So, while design thinking gave us a framework, it's clear we need more than that. We need a mindset that goes beyond solving problems for the present and looks to anticipate future needs. We must design with intention, humility and a broader sense of responsibility. At the end of the day, the world doesn't need more things — it needs better.

Becoming a designer at 35 and picking up a new skill felt monumental, but began quite small — with a blog post I wanted to write, but didn't have a blog to post it on. So, in 2009, I set up my first Blogger page. However, as someone stepping into the design world, the Blogger aesthetics didn't cut it for me — to be blunt, they looked terrible. I needed something that reflected my budding identity as a designer, so decided to design my own site.

At that time, I was living in Brighton, a bayside suburb of Melbourne, while my daughter Mia (Miff) had just started school at Brighton Primary. My evenings were consumed by crafting my website, and I remember for Father's Day that year Miff came home with a drawing that put things into perspective for me. She had drawn my round bald head, a computer screen, a set of curtains, and a caption that read, 'My dad is amazing; he stares at his computer all night and likes to look out the window. He never goes out; he is very clever'. Sometimes, the simple observations from kids deliver the most profound insights.

After many late nights, I finally built my website and blog from scratch. Now it just needed a name that would reflect my design journey. Intrigued by Google's start, I stumbled on an article detailing how they requested an 'uncluttered white space' for their first office in San Francisco. That phrase struck a chord with me. It encapsulated what I wanted my blog to be — a clean, clear space to document and share my journey into the design world. My blog 'Uncluttered White Space' was born, marking the start of a new chapter in my life where design was no longer just an interest, but something I wrote about, practised and researched.

◊◊◊

'Prototype your life. Try stuff instead of making grand plans.' This piece of wisdom from Kevin Kelly, founding executive editor of *Wired* magazine, was so important to me, especially as someone born in 1975. I often dive into the past, exploring the design and creation of objects around the time I entered the world. It's fascinating to see how ideas birthed back then continue to influence our present.

I've lived through almost five decades now, straddling two millennia of immense change and technological evolution. Yet, years ago, people laid the foundations for many of the things we take for granted today. Early influences, including the people who loved us and those we loved, often serve as the foundational elements of who we are.

The world was a different place in the 1970s and 1980s. We didn't have constant connectivity as we do now. Entertainment and information weren't just a click away. Back then, creativity and effort were necessary to fill our days. We would ride our bikes over to a friend's house just to see if they were free to hang out, and if a new song caught our ear, acquiring it meant a physical trip to the store, sometimes waiting days for the chance.

Growing up as part of generation X, I hold dear the cultural icons of my youth — from the groundbreaking sounds of Nirvana and Pearl Jam to the pop prowess of Madonna and Cyndi Lauper. John Hughes's films, such as *Some Kind of Wonderful*, *Ferris Bueller's Day Off* and *Pretty in Pink* (with Hughes either as writer or writer and director), have influenced our perceptions of adolescence and individuality.

> **Everything around us has been carefully engineered to solve specific challenges... Every design has a purpose, every form a function.**

This obsession with past culture, technologies and designs is about more than nostalgia; it's also about understanding how deeply design is woven into our daily existence. Everything around us has been carefully engineered to solve specific challenges. Have you ever considered why things are designed the way they are? Every design has a purpose, every form a function. Embarking on this kind of retrospective journey can be eye-opening, offering insights into how design shapes our interaction with the world.

# INSIGHTS

The 1970s were a pivotal decade for technological innovation, producing designs that continue to influence our daily lives. Here are five significant inventions from that era:

1. *Personal computer (PC):* Introducing the personal computer revolutionised how we work, communicate and entertain ourselves. The Apple II, launched in 1977, was one of the first successful mass-produced microcomputers. This innovation brought computing into the homes and offices of ordinary people, setting the stage for the digital age.

2. *Mobile phone:* In 1973, Martin Cooper, a Motorola engineer, made the first mobile telephone call from handheld subscriber equipment, laying the groundwork for the cell phones we rely on today. This technology has evolved from bulky, limited-range devices to sophisticated smartphones that are powerful computing tools.

3. *Digital camera:* Steve Sasson at Kodak invented the first digital camera in 1975. This innovation eventually changed the photography industry, shifting it from analogue to digital, and impacting both professional photography and the daily lives of general consumers by making photo-taking and sharing instantaneous.

4. *MRI scanner:* The development of magnetic resonance imaging (MRI) technology in the late 1970s was a significant advancement in medical diagnostics. MRI scanners use magnetic fields and radio waves to create detailed images of the organs and tissues in the body. This tool has become crucial for non-invasive medical diagnostics, improving the accuracy of diagnoses.

5. *Fibre optics:* While researchers explored the principle earlier, they made significant advancements in using optical fibres for communication in the 1970s. These developments led to high-speed internet connectivity, forming the backbone of global communications infrastructure and enabling myriad applications, from broadband internet access to medical instruments.

These inventions represented a breakthrough in their respective fields and laid the foundation for further innovations that now define contemporary life. The 1970s' legacy in shaping today's technological landscape is profound, demonstrating the lasting impact of that decade's spirit of innovation.

Three designs from my youth continue to fascinate and inspire me: the Betamax, the Walkman and Steven Sasson's Kodak digital camera.

Sony's Betamax video cassette tape, designed by the inventive Nobutoshi Kihara, an engineer at Sony and known affectionately as 'Mr. Walkman', was a technical wonder in the realm of home entertainment during its time. In all likelihood, Kihara employed oscilloscopes to visualise electrical signals and early circuit simulators to test the designs before constructing physical prototypes. Creating these prototypes would have involved meticulous sketches on tracing paper, varying the hardness of pencils to refine the details, followed by crafting wood or foam models to complete the physical form of the Betamax.

Betamax offered unmatched picture quality compared to its rival VHS. Despite its technical superiority, however, Betamax remains a classic example of a superior product overtaken by market dynamics. VHS was able to win over consumers with longer recording times and more affordable pricing—factors that proved decisive in the consumer market.

# INSIGHTS

Nobutoshi Kihara was a pioneering Japanese engineer whose innovative spirit and technical prowess left a mark on the world. Kihara was a key figure at Sony, where he played a significant role in developing some of the company's most iconic products.

Born in 1926, Kihara joined Sony in 1952, when the company was still a start-up. Because of his exceptional engineering and problem-solving skills, he became an integral part of Sony's development team. Kihara's past work involved improving tape recorder technologies, which were critical during the 1950s and 1960s.

However, his most famous contribution came in 1979 when he invented the Sony Walkman, a portable cassette player that revolutionised the way people listened to music. The concept of the Walkman came about when Sony's co-founder, Masaru Ibuka, wanted a more private way to listen to opera music during his frequent international flights. Kihara took on this challenge, transforming the existing bulky tape recorder technology into a compact, battery-operated and headphone-equipped device that allowed individuals to listen to music on the go.

The Walkman was not just a technical achievement; it was a cultural phenomenon that forever changed music consumption. It made personal music listening a part of everyday life and paved the way for future portable electronic devices such as MP3 players and smartphones.

By the end of production in 2010, Sony had sold 20 million cassette-type Walkman devices. Sony's digital Walkman devices such as DAT, MiniDisc, CD Walkman (originally Discman), and memory-type media players have sold 400 million.

Kihara remained at Sony until retirement, leaving behind a legacy of creativity and invention that inspires engineers and designers worldwide.

The design and engineering world in 1975 embraced manual processes and the tactile feel of physical tools. Steve Sasson, a visionary engineer at the Eastman Kodak Company (Kodak), epitomised this era with his groundbreaking work on the first digital camera. Crafting this early technology was a labour-intensive process. Sasson had to draft schematics by hand with careful precision, using tools such as French curves for smooth arcs and various protractors for precise angles. Each part of the camera, from the intricate circuit board to the robust outer casing, was shaped by Sasson's meticulous attention to detail and the skilled hands of his committed team.

Steve Sasson, who turned 76 in 2024, is now a celebrated figure in technology for his invention of the digital camera. However, the journey to this groundbreaking achievement could have been smoother. Within Kodak, Sasson faced considerable scepticism. Imagine the scene in the mid-1970s: Sasson presents a bulky device, about the size of a toaster, that takes a painfully slow 23 seconds to 'snap' a photo, which could then only be displayed on a television screen. The Kodak executives were underwhelmed, and their reactions ranged from dismissive to patronising, with comments like, 'That's cute — but don't tell anyone about it.' This initial resistance is a stark reminder that even the most revolutionary innovations can be met with doubt and dismissal.

Despite the lack of enthusiasm, Sasson persisted with his work on the digital camera, operating almost like a covert skunkworks project within Kodak. He continued refining the technology unnoticed as Kodak focused on its then-lucrative film business. This digital camera, revolutionary as it was, remained a footnote in Kodak's extensive patent library for years. It wasn't until the rise in demand for digital photography and the technological advancements in the late 1990s and early 2000s that the true potential of Sasson's work became evident. By this time, however, Kodak had lost its chance to be a first mover in digital photography (with Canon launching the first commercially available digital camera in 1986), becoming a cautionary tale of a corporate giant caught flat-footed by its groundbreaking innovation.

# INSIGHTS

In 1888, George Eastman established Kodak as the Eastman Kodak Company, marking the beginning of a revolutionary era in photography. Eastman's philosophy was simple yet transformative: make photography accessible to everyone by making it as convenient as using a pencil. His innovations in film development and introduction of the Kodak camera, which came preloaded with enough film for 100 exposures, were pivotal in turning photography into a household activity.

For most of the 20th century, Kodak dominated the photographic film market. The company's success was due to its continued innovations in photography and aggressive marketing and business strategies. Kodak developed a lucrative business model known as the 'razor and blades', where it sold cameras at a low cost to boost the sale of its highly profitable film rolls.

However, Kodak was late to acknowledge the shift in consumer preference towards digital photography. By the time it did, the company struggled to gain a significant foothold in the market. Kodak's profits dwindled as film sales declined, and despite attempts to diversify its portfolio, the company needed help to recover its commanding presence.

In 2012, Kodak filed for Chapter 11 bankruptcy protection, a stark declaration of its decline from a blue-chip giant to a casualty of technological evolution and market shifts. The company emerged from bankruptcy in 2013, focusing on imaging for businesses, including digital printing and enterprise services, but it remains a shadow of its former self.

I love the Kodak story. It illuminates the potential pitfalls of organisational inertia and serves as a cautionary tale about embracing disruptive innovation, even when it threatens existing business models. But we know that already — don't we, Blockbuster!

What I love about design is its simplicity and its problem-solving power. David Kelley, a titan in the design world and one of my heroes, perfectly illustrates this. Picture this: it's the early eighties, and Kelley is on a plane. He gets up to use the restroom, only to find the door locked. A small window on the handle indicates it's occupied. He returns to his seat, waits and then tries again — the same result. Frustrated, he wonders, 'Why can't I just know from my seat if the toilet is occupied?'

This annoyance led Kelley to design a simple yet ingenious solution — a light that passengers could see from their seats to indicate when the restroom was occupied. This innovation, though small, significantly enhanced the flying experience by solving a common inconvenience that had been overlooked since the advent of commercial flights. His design came some 20 years after the introduction of commercial flights.

His portfolio also includes designing the first mouse for Apple, the stand-up toothpaste tube and various medical devices. Kelley's creations stem from a keen observation of everyday problems and a drive to create functional, user-friendly solutions.

## INSIGHTS

Have you ever paused to consider the designs subtly orchestrating your daily life? Beyond the striking architecture or sleek gadgets, overlooked, everyday items often shape our routines. Take a moment to reflect on those silent design heroes around you. Maybe it's a favourite mug that fits snugly in your hands or a well-placed bookshelf that turns a chaotic heap of books into an organised trove of knowledge.

Choose an object or system you interact with daily and peel back the layers of its design story. Ask yourself why it was crafted the way it was. What problem does it solve, and how does it subtly enhance your life? Design is more than mere aesthetics; it's a continuous dialogue between creator and consumer, form and function, problem and solution.

What sprang to mind when I asked you to look at the objects around you? Was it the beach towel beneath you, the couch you're lounging on, or perhaps the device — a Kindle or an iPad — through which you're reading these words? Each was conceived and crafted by someone, somewhere. Discuss these designs with friends; such conversations illuminate the often-unseen creativity surrounding you, the kind that speaks in hushed tones rather than shouts. Acknowledging the quiet innovation that fills your life helps you to view your world as a vast gallery of ingenuity. This perspective can shift your uncertainty about your ideas — toward realising that if these designers could embody their visions into reality, you could too. You too can get your ideas out of your head and into the world.

## INSIGHTS

Creativity is a journey, not a destination. It builds on what came before, improving it, and adapting to new challenges and needs.

Don't aim for perfection — aim for progress. Let each iteration teach you something and guide you toward a better result. The creative process is never truly finished; it's always evolving, always moving forward.

See each ending as a new beginning. Keep creating, keep refining, and let every step bring you closer to making a meaningful impact.

# PART V

# DIRECTIONS: RESILIENCE

### Where creativity is tested and strengthened, building the resilience to adapt and evolve through challenges

Resilience is at the heart of finding the right direction. I've seen many projects stumble and faced my fair share of setbacks. What I've learned is that true creative confidence isn't built on just success but also the willingness to learn, adapt and keep moving forward. Through embracing change you can use each failure as a stepping stone, not a setback. The more you lean into resilience, the more you trust your instincts — knowing you can navigate any challenge that comes your way, any direction.

# CHAPTER 13

# WHERE TO PARK ON YOUR WAY TO THE FUTURE!

Learning how resilience helps guide your creativity forward

In 2018, I purchased an old 1998 Mercedes-Benz Vito, my 'mid-life crisis ski van'. I adored it; Nicola thought it was a parking-space-hogging nightmare — my midlife mic drop. I threw down five grand for it at 43, not as a crisis purchase, but as a declaration. The van I'd always wanted, with mag wheels and tinted windows, was a small rebellion against the 'shoulds' and 'musts' that come with adulting. I decked it out with a bed in the back, a bench seat, ski racks, a surfboard shelf that held two mals and a few drawers — nothing too fancy, just something that said, 'Yeah, I'm the guy who craves a bit of adventure'. I wasn't trying to turn back time but I was hoping to stir up that part of me that yearned for the open road and the thrill of what's around the next bend. At least, that is my excuse.

One day, Nicola squeezed it into a spot, taking our eagle-eyed seven-year-old Pip shopping in Jindabyne in the NSW Alpine region. Pip is our clever child — really clever — and much brighter than kids number one and two (don't worry, they won't read this).

Coming back to the car, Pip spotted a note under the windscreen. Nicola sees this as another lesson for Pip to expand her reading skills.

'Oh, how exciting, Pip! Why don't you read it out?' Nicola encouraged. 'What does it say, munchkin?'

Pip squinted, deciphering the handwriting with her seven-year-old brain, and stuttered out slowly,

'It says, "You park like a shit c**t!"'

The world's least subtle critique of my wife's parking and Pip's newest addition to her first-grade vocabulary.

# INSIGHTS

From my earliest memories, I've been drawn to the allure of the old and the well-worn. This fascination with antiques was a thread woven through my life, inspired by my mum's passion for exploring quaint little antique shops during our family drives from Sydney to Dubbo. Each dusty shelf and every gleaming trinket told a story—stories of past lives and eras that captured my imagination. Who had cherished this piece? What secret histories did it hold?

This wasn't merely about collecting objects; it was also about collecting stories, embracing the charm of the overlooked and the undervalued. This early love for the past's narratives would profoundly influence my professional path, steering me towards embracing and reshaping these stories to innovate for the future. Each antique was a lesson in design and history, a tangible link to when each item was crafted with intention and purpose.

My connection to the past, especially to music and cars, has profoundly shaped my relationship with my son, Kai. As he grew up, we bonded over classic tunes and the stories behind them. On road trips, Nicola and I made a point of not just playing music but also discussing the artists and the history behind each song. We wanted to humanise the music for our kids, and show them that these were great melodies as well as pieces of history echoing through time, written by someone, somewhere, real people, just like them. This approach fostered a deep family appreciation for country music, most importantly for the stories it told. I shared with them my mother's love for icons such as Dolly Parton, Kenny Rogers and Loretta Lynn, and how their songs were narratives of life's complexities. Even Marty Robbins' *Gunfighter Ballads and Trail Songs* found its place in our journeys, illustrating how old tunes can bridge generations.

Similarly, Kai and I connected through our shared fascination with car designs. Despite knowing nothing technical about cars, their aesthetics captivated us. We spent hours poring over images of classics such as the DeLorean and the mid-1980s Ford F150 and Bronco, marvelling at their distinctive shapes and features, including bench seats and column shifts. We even followed online articles about people who reimagined these vintage models, dreaming up our versions.

The love for design and storytelling wasn't confined to Kai and me; it also extended to my daughters, who were drawn to the visual arts. They grew up sketching faces and sea life, translating their visions onto paper. When my mother passed away, Miff and Pip created a portrait that captured her essence. The piece now hangs proudly in our family home, serving as a poignant reminder of our shared stories and memories.

Kai's journey into music blossomed from this foundation. One afternoon, at 15, Kai came home from school and asked if we could take him to the pub that night. My first reaction was a mix of amusement and surprise. 'Mate', I said, 'you're supposed to sneak out to the pub, not ask your mum and dad to take you'.

'No, Dad,' he replied. 'There's an open mic night at the pub. I have a few songs I want to sing. Can you drive me up at 8 pm?'

My wife and I exchanged puzzled looks. We knew Kai had been playing guitar since he was five, but singing? This was new territory. 'Are you sure, mate? We're happy to take you. I bet you'd be amazing, but Helensburgh pub is full of grown men from the local mines. Are you sure that's your audience?'

'Yeah, Dad, that's my audience. Thanks!'

So, we drove him to the pub at 8 pm. He walked in and set up his guitar with his lifelong guitar teacher and local friend, Peter Jordan. They plugged in, and Kai started to sing. He performed a cover of Zach Bryan's 'Something in the Orange', Bush's 'Glycerine', and a song by Oasis.

I must admit, I knew a few locals and was nervously perched by the door, ready for a quick escape if things went south. I couldn't help but think, *Holy shit, what if he sings like me?* But as soon as he started, it was clear — Kai could sing, and he sang beautifully.

Since that night, our home is often filled with his songs. Written in the confines of his bedroom, they now flow into the dining room and out to the pub for locals to enjoy. Over the years, he has sung to friends and family, and his performances have made my heart swell with pride. At just 15, Kai found his voice and started earning money singing solo in pubs and leading school plays. He found his voice through shared stories and songs, showing how our connections to the past shape our present and future.

## INSIGHTS

In our family, storytelling and creativity are intertwined. Each generation draws from the old to inspire the new, weaving a continuous thread through music, art and design. This legacy of creativity, rooted in the past yet vibrantly alive in the present, is a testament to the enduring power of storytelling and the deep connections it fosters.

Long before the 1998 Vito, I bought an old 1989 Holden Rodeo ute for the price of a pair of sunglasses and $1750 from my mate, Dave Tanner. It was a trusty, rugged companion for my surfboards and mountain bikes, sporting rust, dents and bumps like badges of honour. Despite its battered condition, the column shift and the old bench seat gave it a nostalgic charm. It may have looked like a wreck, but I loved that ute until the day it finally gave out four years later.

In 2012, shortly after acquiring my vintage ute, my business at the time, 6.2, faced a formidable task from Unigas, a German enterprise specialising in the autogas industry: how could we make autogas — a type of liquefied petroleum gas (LPG) — a universally appealing alternative to petrol and diesel? Autogas had a somewhat undeserved reputation at the time, and was often confined to powering taxis, trucks and commercial fleets. However, when examined through the lens of environmental impact, autogas has some clear benefits, releasing fewer greenhouse gases and volatile organic compounds than its more popular fossil fuel counterparts — petrol and diesel.

The problem we were trying to solve was twofold. Autogas had already been extracted and was sitting in storage tanks — with a staggering 60-year reserve just in Australia. It was also begging for a second chance, much like the forgotten treasures I'd seek with my mum during childhood road trips. As we faced the challenge of repositioning autogas, we couldn't help but see its untapped potential with 60 years of energy in storage. Our mission was to rebrand and elevate autogas as a transitional fuel that could serve as a stepping stone towards a more sustainable future, providing a 'less bad' alternative. The world is moving towards electric and hydrogen-based solutions. With 60 years of this fuel already extracted and stored, the question arose: could this stored energy serve as an immediate, yet temporary, solution until more sustainable options become widely accessible? We now had a well-defined problem statement.

We considered an 'influencer road trips' campaign, where trusted voices could narrate their firsthand experience of using autogas while traversing Australia's beautiful landscapes. Education was another cornerstone; envisaging partnerships with academic institutions, we thought of developing curriculums and R&D initiatives that could validate autogas as a viable fuel alternative.

From a financial standpoint, conversion subsidies and mileage-based rewards were also considered potential incentives. A complementary mobile app designed to locate autogas stations and provide real-time data on environmental savings could serve as both a utility and an educational tool.

One of the most compelling of our considered propositions was the revolutionary idea of a hybrid prototype car that ran on electric and autogas. This would move us beyond bridging technologies and championing autogas as a viable transitional fuel until sustainable solutions became commonplace. Our concept would create the world's most affordable, lightweight and compact car, designed uniquely for autogas.

But the real magic was in its customisability. Picture changing your car's bonnet as effortlessly as swapping your smartphone case — from a Union Jack to an eight-ball design, perhaps. We pared down the dashboard to its essentials, allowing a smartphone to integrate seamlessly and take over as the control hub for everything from tracking speed to monitoring fuel consumption.

The windows could pop out for those sunny days, and the roof quickly clipped off, stashing away neatly for an open-air experience. Even the air conditioning was innovatively simple, relying purely on the rush of outside air filtered through a unit as the car moved. This car wasn't just a mode of transport; it was a statement on the future of automotive design.

While these were just ideas, they had the power to change both policy and perception. Of course, what Unigas ultimately chose to implement remains confidential. Still, our aim was precise: highlight autogas as a stepping stone in transitioning to cleaner, more sustainable energy solutions. We wanted to tell a story where this overlooked fuel could have its moment as a transitional fuel.

The ideas were compelling and, for me, they still are today.

Soon after submitting these ideas, we were summoned for a high-level discussion with Unigas executives in Sydney.

I took the ute to get to the meeting because I wanted to stop for a surf. In a moment steeped in irony, I pulled into the Unigas facility, driving my beat-up 1989 Holden Rodeo ute, complete with surfboard and wetsuit in the back.

The security boom gate lowered before me, acting like a guardian to the facility and the industry's future. I made a brief phone call to Cam, our client, who was standing with his executive team nearby. I introduced myself by saying, 'Hey Cam, I can't enter the boom gate.' The boom gate seemed to rise in slow motion as Cam and his team watched in doubt as I drove in, calculating the odds of our venture's success in real time.

As we sat in the boardroom, I could almost hear them thinking out loud — was this guy in the shit box ute a red flag, or was this an indication that he was the kind of out-of-the-box thinker they needed? Their faces seemed caught between amusement and existential dread. My battered ute wasn't just rolling into a parking space; it was crashing through preconceptions. How could this guy be on the pathway? What were they expecting, a BMW X5?

## INSIGHTS

With its contrasting layers, this meeting was a turning point for me. It later influenced Reny's transformation into a B Corp, and prompted a profound re-evaluation of our environmental responsibilities. Before this experience, my engagement with ecological issues had been on the periphery. However, from that day onward, my focus underwent a significant shift. Social and environmental considerations ceased to be mere sidelines; they became central to our operations.

When we started 6.2, we wanted to help small businesses. That shifted over time, and we became a business that would work for and assist anyone with a bank account. We moved away from our roots onto big brands and companies, and not because they had an internist or significant problem to solve but just because they sent us a brief.

After the Unigas project and around the time of walking out of 6.2 in 2016, I had to rethink. During our four years chasing the snow, Nicola and I created our manifesto and framework for who we wanted to work for. And sure, it didn't rule anyone out; we could continue to work for companies like Unigas, and we do work to this day that we are very proud of for companies such as the John Holland Group. However, the work we chose to do for them must matter. It needs to change something, improve something. We now ask ourselves, 'Is this work intentional and valuable?'

Around the same time, Nicola joined Reny as our ESG (environmental, social and governance) Manager, collaborating with charitable partners dedicated to environmental causes, such as the Surfrider Foundation, Balu Blue, 1% for the Planet and Patagonia, as well as health-focused partners such as the Heart Foundation, Skin Check Champions, Beard Season and Cancer Council.

Before transitioning into an impact-led agency, our partnerships with these brands and environmental causes needed to be more prominent. We used to seek commercial work, but our shift at Reny to a Good Company policy redirected our focus toward impact and intention, and then clients who shared our values began seeking us out. Whether reducing carbon footprints, making sustainable choices or selecting clients who align with our commitment to a better future, every aspect of our work reflects our dedication to positive change.

Like that old ute, sometimes the overlooked things have the most valuable lessons to teach us. The key to unlocking potential lies in embracing the unexpected, a lesson I learned early while exploring those little shops with my mum. It's a principle that has served me well throughout my professional journey. When Nicola assumed the ESG Manager role, something changed — a work felt more rewarding. In our way, we were contributing to changing the world.

Here's our Good Company statement, beautifully crafted by my Nicola Rennie:

> *The Good Company is our way of building a design agency for humanity. Technology is transforming the way we interact with the world, and we strive to use it to create positive shifts. We acknowledge challenges like climate change, inequality and*

*environmental degradation. We are committed to being part of the solution by using our Good Company policy to promote social and environmental stability. We aspire to be the best design agency we can be for humanity.*

And now, here we are, at the crossroads of ideas. This is where we transform well-defined problems into actionable solutions. Where do these ideas come from? Let go of the notion that you need to be a creative genius. Sometimes, the best ideas spring from rearranging existing pieces and envisioning how they could fit together in new ways. These ideas are sparks that transform a 'problem' into an 'opportunity for change'.

> **Let go of the notion that you need to be a creative genius. Sometimes, the best ideas spring from rearranging existing pieces and envisioning how they could fit together in new ways.**

Ideas are guided by 'what if?' in work and life. What if we approached the problem from this angle? What if we provided users with a more straightforward yet more meaningful solution? I see this as being like having a sketchbook where I connect dots on the map of the problem. Some lines are straight, some are curvy and others meander, but they all lead to potential solutions that can be tested, refined and used.

# INSIGHTS

It's easy to become an expert in listing constraints—time, money or talent scarcity, for example—but what if those constraints are the secret sauce to spur creativity? What if you viewed them not as insurmountable obstacles but as the sparks that ignite innovation?

Constraints can act as invisible boundaries, inviting you to rethink your approach, find loopholes and resilience, and unlock opportunities. They don't always limit creativity; they can challenge you to see problems differently and transform obstacles into stepping stones for new perspectives. When that inner voice warns you of limitations, listen closely—it's a call to lean in and push through. The best ideas often emerge when you navigate those boundaries.

On 18 October 2021, just a few months before the 2022 Beijing Winter Olympics (held in February 2022), Miff's world turned upside down. She was skiing in Livigno, Italy, training with the Australian team. Before her knee buckled, she executed a clean 360-degree spin on a simple wind-down session. Miff was whisked away to Zurich for medical attention, hoping it was a minor injury. Unfortunately, it wasn't. Deep into the COVID-19 pandemic as we all were at the time, Nicola and I were back home in Australia. Miff, then 17, was travelling with her coach, Leon Tarbotton, who took her to see specialists for scans and assessments. They confirmed the worst, and the diagnosis was devastating: a torn meniscus, posterior and anterior cruciate ligament (PCL and ACL) and lateral collateral ligament (LCL).

The Australian ski team's medical staff were occupied at another event in France, leaving Miff to fend for herself in Switzerland for the next three days. Leon, Miff's coach since she was 13, stepped up to ensure she received the necessary care. Without the right equipment to assess her knee, the medical team in Switzerland put her into a full-length cast. Due to the global pandemic restrictions, she couldn't immediately return home due to Australian lockdown and hotel quarantine policies. If she did fly back, Miff would have to sit in a hotel for two weeks — isolated with a shattered knee, unable to receive proper care. The decision was made to instead wait it out in Switzerland. After 15 days, Miff finally flew back to Australia. Her Olympic dreams were shattered.

On Miff's return, we met with surgeons and specialists. With a recommendation from good friends Dave and Liza Kelly, Miff entrusted her surgery to Dr Brett Fritsch. The operation went smoothly, and the long road to recovery began.

Eight weeks later, as the Winter Olympic Games loomed, Miff prepared to come to terms with watching her teammates compete from the sidelines, grappling with the reality of her shattered dream. Then she received a call from her good friend and role model, Torah Bright, informing her that the team at Channel 7 were looking for a commentator. A week later, the Channel 7 producer offered her a shot at commentating for the women's freeski and big air events. Miff aced the audition and secured the role, along with hosting Channel 7's live TikTok feed, where each night she would broadcast live interviews with athletes in the village and review the daily results. Miff's TikToks garnered over a billion viewers over the few weeks of the Olympics. Nicola and I watched every night and, along with the interviews and summaries, what we really witnessed was our daughter kicking the absolute shit out of plan B with grace and resilience.

Constraints had thrown Miff's Olympic journey off course, but she didn't let them derail her dreams. Her ability to adapt and find new opportunities is a testament to the power of determination, creativity and resilience—qualities that transform boundaries into fresh beginnings. One door closes, another opens.

In *The Last Policeman*, author Ben H Winters crafts a world teetering on the brink of collapse as humanity faces certain destruction from an impending asteroid impact six months in the future. Against this apocalyptic backdrop, the book's main character, Detective Hank Palace, remains committed to solving crimes, even as society crumbles around him. While many surrender to despair and abandon their responsibilities, Hank Palace persists in pursuing truth, seeking justice for those who have been forgotten amid the chaos.

Palace's resolve sets a powerful scene for adapting creative solutions in the most dire of real-world settings: the world's end! Despite external pressure and imminent catastrophe (the end of the world), he draws meaning and purpose from his work, refusing to yield to hopelessness. He embodies the principle that persistence, resilience, adaptability and creativity can still uncover value and resolve unexpectedly, even when the task ahead seems impossible, indifferent or useless.

As Palace navigates the bleak landscape, he uncovers opportunities for truth and resolution that others fail to see. Even when the world turns dark, his purpose shines a little light.

**Challenges force us to reimagine things, create ingenuity, find fresh perspectives and discover new solutions that shift our perceived limitations.**

Each story in this chapter—from Kai's journey into music to Miff's ability to pivot gracefully to her 'plan B', and from the autogas challenge to the determined resolve of Detective Palace in *The Last Policeman*—is a testament to the power of resilience. Resilience is what drives us to adapt, to see possibilities where others see obstacles and to create something meaningful despite constraints. It's in these moments of pressure—when the path forward seems uncertain—that creativity truly shines. These stories remind us that resilience isn't just about weathering the storm; it's about using the storm as fuel to innovate, thrive and uncover new directions we never thought possible.

Resilience helps us transform setbacks into opportunities. Through adaptability, curiosity and a commitment to purpose, resilience becomes the spark that ignites innovation and helps us navigate life's unexpected twists, uncovering new paths we might never have imagined.

Challenges force us to reimagine things, create ingenuity, find fresh perspectives and discover new solutions that shift our perceived limitations.

Creative adaptability isn't just a response to adversity—it's a crucial skill that lets us thrive amid challenges, be resilient and make a difference, setting us on a path we never saw coming.

## INSIGHTS

Your quirks aren't flaws—they're your creative superpowers. The very things that set you apart can spark your best ideas. So stop trying to fit in and start embracing what makes you uniquely you.

True creativity comes when you own your oddities and bring your unique perspective to the table. When you let yourself create without holding back, the real breakthroughs happen.

Let your quirks be your compass.

# CHAPTER 14

# STANDARD STANDARDS ARE STANDARD!

Knowing when to follow the rules, and when to break them in the name of creativity

Stephen King once said, 'Monsters are real, and ghosts are real too. They live inside us, and sometimes, they win'. It's a haunting reminder that the biggest battles often aren't against external challenges but the fears, doubts and regrets we carry within. These inner demons — whether they're voices of self-doubt, past failures or the fear of taking risks — can be the most formidable obstacles to creativity and progress. Sometimes, they cloud our vision, slow us down or even convince us to abandon our dreams.

We could have considered abandoning one of the first projects we took on at Reny, but we were determined to find creative solutions instead. To explain, let me take you back to the beginning of the venture ...

The world has enough socks. Sure, it has enough books, too. So the question arises: why produce more? But this is where a crucial distinction lies — it's not about creating *more*, but *better*. Sportswear Company Chair Carlo Rivetti, who I talk about in chapter 8, profoundly influenced this perspective, instilling in me the ethos of crafting things with purpose, integrity and sustainability.

Carlo's lessons helped me navigate a world cluttered with products. I've filled my home with things I cherish — Nike sneakers that trace back to my teenage years, a vintage watch that ticks tales and picture frames that are windows to my family's soul. But my fascination isn't so much with possessions as with the stories and impact of the items we choose to surround ourselves with.

In 2018, I was lucky to cross paths with Jarryd Williams, an Australian snowboarder turned entrepreneur who ventured into the niche of creating quality socks for skateboarders, snowboarders and the everyday adventurer. His brand, Standard Sock Co, was born from passion and partnership, but had hit a standstill as his co-founders scattered across the globe.

Sitting in a cosy corner of Mt Buller, over the comforting clink of cold beers, Jarryd and I discussed the future of his fledgling sock company. We both wanted to reignite the brand with potential. With a robust design team behind me and extensive experience in brand management, taking over this little sock company seemed less about business and acquisition, and more about stewardship. Over the years, I'd seen businesses rise and fall. I'd spearheaded projects that soared and some that sank without a trace. Here was now an opportunity to apply all those lessons to something as simple yet essential as socks. Here was my chance to infuse a small brand with grand ideas of quality and innovation.

So, we agreed with a handshake in the chilly air of a snow-dusted evening. Nicola and I would take the reins of this sock brand, driven not just by the prospect of profit but also by the promise of creating something worthwhile that could stand the test of time and tread.

This passing of the Standard Sock Co torch from our friends in Melbourne lit the way for Nicola to step into a role she was born to fill — leading a project with innovation and sustainability at its heart. Our (at the time, ongoing) globetrotting sabbatical had deepened our respect for the environment, reshaping our perspectives. We realised that the world didn't need more socks; it needed better socks. Nicola was determined to revolutionise the idea of what socks could be, setting a new standard for how they could impact the world positively.

Nicola's mission was to create the world's most sustainable snowboarding sock — a bold and inspiring goal. Redefining something as fundamental as socks is no small feat, however. So she reached out to professional surfer Kelly Slater for advice, and he was gracious with his support, sharing his insights from Outerknown, his sustainable clothing brand, and pointing Nicola in the right direction. Nicola also connected with Eric Crane, the co-founder and CEO of Electric Eyewear in California, who provided further guidance and encouragement.

Nicola's vision began to take shape after countless brainstorming sessions, meticulous design refinements and 35 distinct prototypes. Her focus on the circular economy — creating a system that eliminates waste by reusing materials and minimising environmental impact — became the cornerstone of the brand. She wasn't simply adding another sock to the market; she was crafting a symbol of sustainable innovation.

Nicola envisioned a 'closed-loop' system where worn-out socks could be recycled into new products, reducing waste and extending the life of every fibre. Each material, stitch and seam was thoughtfully selected, ensuring that the final product was a testament to creativity, care and a better way forward. The Standard Sock Co wasn't just a sock company; it was also a commitment to better design and a beacon for sustainable practices in the fashion industry.

## INSIGHTS

The manufacturing industry often overlooks its water footprint, which is crucial in evaluating environmental impact. While some materials may be touted for their eco-friendliness, the reality of production can sometimes tell a different story. Most manufacturing processes involve significant water usage, and harsh chemical treatments can render the water non-reusable, posing severe environmental threats. Producing one standard T-shirt, for example, can consume up to 2700 litres of water, roughly the amount an average person drinks over three years or the equivalent of 70 showers.

Bamboo was initially celebrated as a sustainable alternative to cotton due to its rapid growth and minimal pesticide need. However, while growing bamboo is sustainable, transforming it into textiles is not. Substantial amounts of water and chemicals are required to break the bamboo into usable fabric, a process fraught with environmental hazards. The water is contaminated with chemicals and cannot be used again. It goes to waste.

Nicola, committed to genuinely sustainable practices, saw a critical opportunity to innovate within the circular economy. She created socks that exemplified minimal ecological impact, choosing materials thoughtfully. Her line used recovery yarns, Tencel fibres (made from wood), upcycled carpets and recycled cotton — all selected for their low environmental toll and potential for reuse. Her production practices aimed to repurpose and reintegrate resources, minimising waste.

(continued)

A further crucial part of Nicola's strategy was rethinking water use in manufacturing. Keeping with her 'closed-loop' approach, she aimed for a system where the water used in production could be treated and reused rather than discarded. This approach reduced the water footprint of each pair of socks and set a new standard in the industry for resource efficiency.

In these ways, the Standard Sock Co was pioneering a model for sustainable manufacturing that could inspire change across the sector.

Nicola collaborated with the London-based environmental production agency SupplyCompass to manufacture the sock. Their dedication to the circular economy aligned perfectly with Nicola's vision for sustainable socks. Together, they chose a Portuguese manufacturer that prioritised responsible production practices and precise craftsmanship. The manufacturer's environmental commitment and ethical working conditions made them the perfect partner.

Nearly two years in the making, our journey culminated with a store launch in June 2020, following trade show pre-orders from September 2019. Based on these pre-orders, we only produced what we needed, reducing waste further and ensuring a focused, sustainable start. With 35 Australian retailers on board, including Larry Adler Ski & Outdoor in Australia and Rhythm Snowsports in Australia and Japan, and partnerships secured with snow resorts Perisher and Thredbo, the market re-entry for the Standard Sock Co showed promise. This solid start was due to our distribution collaboration with our good friend Steve Fisher, owner and director at Sportfactor in Sydney.

Jarryd Williams and his original team had built a stunning brand for Standard Sock Co, with an iconic wombat logo and thoughtfully crafted brand assets. The foundation was solid, and the connection to the market was undeniable. When the launch came in June and July of 2020, the sell-through reflected this strong brand presence and the appeal of Nicola's innovations, creating a promising base to build from.

But... why does there always seem to be a 'but'? In our case, the 'but' was a huge one we hadn't anticipated. After all my years in design, strategy, branding and business, this one stung more than most.

Let's talk about the name for a second: 'Standard'. Sounds good, right? Now, consider the category we were working in: socks. Again, it sounds fine on the surface. But now think about the concept of 'standard sizing' in socks and the global footwear industry. Every major shoe brand makes socks, and countless smaller brands have innovated their take on what a 'standard sock' should be. Nike, Adidas, Puma, Dr. Martens and others all have their own branded socks, including their versions of 'standard' ones.

Naturally, we assumed a firm name like Standard Sock Co would stand out, but the reality was quite the opposite. We became lost online in a sea of digital 'standard' socks. Every search returned socks from big names such as Nike and Adidas, leaving our Standard Sock Co hidden behind their massive presence.

We remained invisible even after partnerships on platforms such as Amazon, Walmart, The Iconic and SurfStitch. Two years and countless hours later, a search for 'Standard Sock Co' on Amazon still returned every other brand's 'standard socks' above ours.

We even worked with an Amazon account manager for six months, but even they couldn't help us break through. Their advice? 'Just change your name.'

Sure enough, a name change became inevitable, so we put our heads together and brainstormed endlessly, creating new names such as Carta, Rennie, Vert, Kcos and Pips. We wanted something searchable and fun. But as we finally settled on a name, COVID-19 struck in earnest, and the world stopped spinning. For us, that meant Standard Sock Co stopped spinning, too, with the 35 stores who had ordered from us in September 2019 cancelling their 2020 orders, regardless of the previous season's success. The pandemic brought a 'last in, first out' mentality, and Standard Sock Co was no exception. Years of work suddenly came crashing to a standstill.

## INSIGHTS

As creators and innovators, we sometimes become prisoners of our prior choices. Seth Godin reminds us that past efforts should never hinder future potential. Our experience with Standard Sock Co became a lesson not only in product design but also in brand identity, naming and, in some ways, humility. It was a stark reminder that even the things we excel at can hold hidden challenges that force us to adapt and rethink our strategies.

*(continued)*

In our pursuit to redefine the sock industry, we learned a critical lesson about balancing innovation and visibility. Crafting an exceptional product is just the beginning; ensuring it works in the vast digital marketplace is the real challenge. Nicola's creation, the world's most sustainable snowboarding sock, was a marvel of eco-design, but its impact could have been better with the right name.

I often advise my clients, 'Done is better than perfect'. This mantra emphasises the importance of progress over perfection. However, our journey with Standard Sock Co taught us that, sometimes, 'done' itself presents a unique set of challenges. The actual test of innovation is in both the creation and the ability to adapt and pivot when necessary. You need to know when to push forward, when to iterate and when to overhaul—like when a name change becomes essential. In our case, we needed to cherish what we've built, while also being open to rebuilding when the situation demanded.

> **People with a flair for creative confidence are distinguishable by their initiative. They don't merely drift with the tide; they set their course, crafting their narrative and imprinting their mark on the world around them.**

People with a flair for creative confidence are distinguishable by their initiative. They don't merely drift with the tide; they set their course, crafting their narrative and imprinting their mark on the world around them. While many might be content staying in the background, individuals like these operate on an 'act now' philosophy. Convinced of the ripple effect their actions can generate, they don't wait for all the stars to align. Instead, they set things in motion, navigating challenges with an adaptable spirit and an enduring optimism.

'Survivorship bias' is a trap that distorts our perception by focusing only on those who made it through, obscuring the lessons hidden in the shadows. This is not a theoretical issue; it's a real-world problem that affects how we interpret business, innovation and achievement.

In business, we marvel at tech giants such as Apple and Amazon, dissecting their strategies to emulate their success while ignoring countless others who took similar paths but didn't survive. This distorted view gives us a false sense of what it takes to win and underestimates the role of luck, timing and market forces.

Innovation faces a similar bias. We celebrate the Edisons and Einsteins but forget those who, despite their brilliance, were hampered by a lack of resources, poor timing or just bad luck. This leaves us with an incomplete narrative about how innovation works.

One of the best examples of survivorship bias comes from World War II. Analysts argued they should reinforce the damaged sections of returning planes, assuming these areas were where the planes were more likely to be hit and so represented weak points. But Abraham Wald noticed the error — these sections were where the planes had sustained non-fatal hits. Instead, they should strengthen the undamaged areas because those were where the fatal hits occurred (on the planes that hadn't returned). This insight saved countless lives and was a crucial reminder to look beyond the survivors.

In business and life, acknowledging survivorship bias helps you craft better strategies. You can gain a nuanced view of risks and rewards by understand your failures. Success is more than luck or genius — it's about understanding the whole picture.

Starting again and picking up the pieces with Standard Sock Co after COVID-19 was hard, and the brand never really made its way back. Bravery often feels like it's for other people, a superpower only the heroic few possess. But that's a misconception. Bravery is simply a choice. Whether standing up for a friend, making a tough decision or sharing a vulnerable idea, you've shown courage before.

You don't need to leap tall buildings or saving the world to show bravery; it's about acting despite the uncertainty. The only question is this: will it be today?

# INSIGHTS

Creativity isn't about following the rules; it's about knowing when to break them. The same standards that shape an industry can sometimes limit your potential. Real innovation happens when you recognise that it's time to disrupt the norm in the name of progress.

Don't shy away from pivoting when things don't go as planned. Your initial idea might not align perfectly with reality, but that's not a setback — it's an opportunity. Embrace change and let it reshape your creative process.

Be bold enough to rewrite the rules when needed.

# CHAPTER 15

# THE ADJACENT POSSIBLE

Pushing the boundaries of what's possible
by staying resilient

As I scroll through certain posts on Instagram and TikTok, nostalgia from that golden era of the 1980s hits me like a wave. I remember the thrill of getting my first Mongoose BMX — it was pure magic. And my waterproof Walkman? Clipping that onto my shorts, I felt like I could conquer the world, with my favourite tunes as my soundtrack.

In 1984, the Transformers toy line also burst onto the scene, with the 'robots in disguise' sparking endless imaginative battles between Autobots and Decepticons. The animated *Transformers* TV series aired around the same time, making Saturday mornings sacred, dedicated to this and other epic cartoons such as *G.I. Joe, ThunderCats* and *He-Man*. My brother and I would sit there, cereal bowls in hand, eyes glued to the screen.

Life seemed simpler back then, with the streets serving as our endless playground. We spent countless hours outside, racing, exploring and crafting our adventures until the streetlights signalled it was time to head home for dinner.

MTV, the cable television network that revolutionised music, started as a 24-hour platform for music videos. It debuted just after midnight on 1 August 1981, with 'Video Killed the Radio Star' by the Buggles. But, for me, MTV came to life in 1985. That was the year my parents officially allowed me to watch it. (Before that, I'd sneakily switch the channel from *The Jetsons* to MTV whenever my parents left the room.) I vividly remember seeing Dire Straits' 'Money for Nothing' video — the electrifying visuals, the raw energy.

Our lounge room in 1985 was the epitome of retro charm: a sunken lounge room with a cream leather lounge, a dial TV with a remote control tethered by a cable and a VHS player nestled against a backdrop of faux brick walls. The carpet, a marled mix of hues, still comes to mind whenever I hear Dire Straits' iconic tune.

Along with the innovations in pop culture, 1985 was a year of vibrant change, blending groundbreaking music, significant political shifts and pivotal global events. In Australia, the airwaves were dominated by Prince, Madonna and Wham!, capturing a world in musical evolution. Politically, figures such as Ronald Reagan, Bob Hawke and Margaret Thatcher were reshaping their nations, navigating economic changes and Cold War tensions. Globally, the Live Aid concerts showcased music's unifying power, rallying aid for the Ethiopian famine. In the Soviet Union, the rise of Mikhail Gorbachev to leader signalled a thaw in East–West relations, hinting at the Cold War's eventual end.

*Back to the Future* captivated moviegoers with its thrilling journey through time, and in my little corner of the world, my life revolved around my Commodore 64. My room became a digital sanctuary, the C64 its centrepiece, surrounded by *Back to the Future* posters that brought a touch of Hollywood magic to my walls. Michael J Fox, with his effortless charm and relentless spirit, became my childhood hero. He continues to inspire me today, reshaping popular culture and our approach to humanity and health with his unyielding fight against Parkinson's disease.

My brother, my best friend Jason Stone and I, just ten years old, ruled over our digital empire within those four walls. Every day after school, we'd dash home, our minds racing with the possibilities of our awaited pixelated escapades. My room was outfitted with a small TV and the C64, and it was our arcade and secret hideaway. The hum of the computer booting up, the click of the joystick and the screen's glow transported us to a place where we were the heroes.

My mum, always encouraging, would often tiptoe in with a tray of popcorn and sodas, infusing our gaming sessions with a cinematic flair. We'd sink into our chairs, as they became the thrones from which we commanded pixels and vanquished virtual foes. The thrill of passing a level or setting a new high score was unmatched. Our imaginations knew no bounds, and every game was a new adventure.

Jason, or Jay as we affectionately called him, was the Commodore's wizard. His secret arsenal included a cigarette lighter he'd rapidly swipe over the joystick buttons. This created a hyperspeed; instead of pressing the left and right buttons with his index and middle finger to gain speed, he would swipe left and right with the lighter. Like I said, hyperspeed! This technique made him a legend in games like 'Hyper Sports'. Records were obliterated, and we watched in awe every time Jay unleashed his skills. He was invincible with a swift wrist movement and a lighter in hand.

The Commodore 64 wasn't just a machine; it was a gateway to other worlds, a spark for friendships and the backdrop to countless childhood memories. And *Back to the Future*? It wasn't merely a movie but a promise of adventures and endless possibilities, perfectly complementing our pixelated quests. In 1985, we didn't just play games or watch films; we lived them.

## INSIGHTS

In the summer of 1982, the Commodore 64 (C64) debuted at US$595, equivalent to US$1880 in 2023. (Competing computers at the time were retailing for over US$1000.) With 17 million units sold between 1983 and 1994, it became the best-selling single personal computer model—and revolutionised personal computing.

What set the C64 apart was its affordability and availability in mainstream retail outlets, and cutting-edge specs. It connected seamlessly to home TVs, a game-changer at the time. Commodore's strategy to produce many parts in-house—and a price war with competitors such as Texas Instruments—meant the consumer price was dropped to US$300 in June 1983, with some stores selling the computer for as low as US$199.

The C64 wasn't just for number-crunching or word processing; it also unleashed creativity with around 10000 commercial software titles available, from development tools to games. It was pivotal in popularising the computer demo scene, showcasing creativity through computer graphics and sound. Even after production ceased in April 1994, the C64's legacy continued through emulators such as VICE, allowing enthusiasts to relive the experience.

*(continued)*

The man behind the iconic C64 was Jack Tramiel, who aimed to democratise computing. His journey from Poland to the US tech industry highlights his foresight and tenacity.

Despite its success, the C64's reign didn't last. As the 1990s approached, new technologies and changing consumer needs outpaced it. The story of the C64 is a tale of innovation, dominance and eventual decline, a standard narrative in the tech industry.

Today, the C64 evokes nostalgia, acting as a reminder of the excitement and potential of computing in its infancy. The C64 wasn't just a machine but also a gateway to a new world and a testament to human ingenuity.

Technology has always played a pivotal role in my life. I recall a clairvoyant predicting a future where I lived near water, had three children and thrived on my fascination with technology. Whether her words influenced me or not, I've always been drawn to how technology shapes lives. This transformative impact even forms the basis of my next book, which delves deep into this subject.

For me, raising kids mirrors the evolution of technology. My mixed emotions connected to the C64's release, and then the engaging Atari and the sophisticated PS5 reflect my journey with my three kids as they grew, each representing a new era of parenting and technology.

My wife and I often joke that our parenting journey can be captured with the evolution of what we call the 'wine glass test'. This lighthearted 'test' shows how our reactions to parenting moments have shifted with each child.

The evening ritual with our firstborn, Miff, back in 2003 was almost sacred. We'd conclude the day, invariably exhausted, pour ourselves some wine and sink into relaxation with our feet propped up. Parenting has always been a monumental challenge for me, profoundly rewarding but incredibly tough. I take immense pride in being a dad and in the kids I've had a hand in raising. But, honestly, Nicola's unwavering guidance, steady presence and the voice of reason kept everything on track, making me feel like a mere apprentice in parenting.

Once we'd tucked Miff in for the night, the unwinding felt like a gentle drift into a dream. We always had plans to relax, but even the softest murmur from the baby monitor — a faint gurgle or burp — would catapult us into high alert. Wine glass hastily set down, we'd be ready to sprint at a moment's notice, hearts thumping, prepared for any emergency, even baby CPR if the situation called for it. We both felt that intuitive, unspoken commitment to parenthood where your child's slightest discomfort triggers an immediate response.

Then along came Kai. With the arrival of our second, our evenings once again involved settling down with a glass of wine, but now, a cough or cry from Kai prompted a brief pause and a knowing glance between us. We'd often finish our glasses, savouring those last sips a bit longer, before quickly checking on him.

By the time Pip entered, our parenting style had evolved quite a bit. Her cries in the night hardly made us cringe. We'd simply look at each other, an unspoken understanding in our eyes, and usually decide to enjoy the rest of the bottle before leisurely making our way to investigate the fuss. Each child brought a new layer to our parenting journey, teaching us that, sometimes, a calm response is just as powerful as a quick one.

This retrospective on our evolving parenting approach isn't merely about how we've adapted to each new challenge; it mirrors the broader journey of growing comfort and confidence. As technology has become more sophisticated and ingrained in our daily lives, so has our approach to raising our kids — shifting from panic to perspective, sprinkled with humour and bound by love. As technology progresses, the essence of our human journey, whether through the latest gadget or a new family member, remains a dynamic, enriching and endlessly intriguing narrative.

## INSIGHTS

Our daily routines are more than just a series of actions; they're part of a larger concept known as 'habitus'. Sociologist Pierre Bourdieu introduced this idea to capture how our subconscious, influenced by culture and society, shapes our thoughts and actions. Our ingrained habits and the surrounding environment create a unique pattern that guides our lives.

*(continued)*

In *Outline of a Theory of Practice*, Bourdieu delved deeply into this concept of habitus, and the idea that our social environments and experiences mould our perceptions and behaviours in ways we often take for granted. He argued that the structures of society are internalised in each of us, influencing our choices and actions without our conscious awareness. This concept highlights the power of our surroundings and their subtle yet profound impact on shaping who we are. By understanding our habits, we can see how our daily routines and environments contribute to our broader life patterns, offering a framework for examining and transforming our lives.

As we examine our habits, we find ourselves at the crossroads of psychology and sociology. From the moment we're born, various forces begin to shape us. These influences range from the pervasive impact of popular culture to the unwritten rules of our communities and the dynamics within our own families. Together, they mould the habits that define us.

Think about the impact of popular culture. More than simply entertainment, it's also a powerful force shaping our worldviews. The movies we watch, the music we listen to and the celebrities we admire do more than helps us pass the time. They act as subtle teachers, shaping our ideas of what's expected and desirable. The heroics of a movie star, the emotional resonance of songs or the glamour of celebrity life influence our thoughts and choices in ways we might not even realise.

Our social environments and communities also play a critical role in shaping our habits. The traditions we follow, the standards we observe and the ways we interact with others are not random. They are deeply ingrained behaviours we've developed over time, often without thinking about them.

When we look deeper into how habits are formed, we discover their stubborn nature, something neuroscience has illuminated. Our brains play a crucial role in this. The brain's reward system reinforces certain behaviours, turning them into habits by creating and reinforcing certain neural pathways. Once a habit is formed, it becomes our default response, making changing or breaking this response challenging.

Habits often work below the surface of our awareness, quietly steering our daily decisions and actions. They significantly impact our lives, shaping everything from minor routines to our most significant life choices. By examining our habits through this lens, we can see how our daily routines and environments contribute to our broader life patterns, offering insights into how we might transform our lives for the better.

This leads me here, to you, and this moment with this book in your hand. I agree with Bourdieu, but I also believe that irrespective of where we are or where we think we are going, everything is a choice — including our circle of friends, our workplace and the food we eat. Sure, habits form these choices but, at the core, they are still choices — and they can be changed.

I write a lot about creativity and advise businesses on design and innovation. But I get my choices wrong — all the time. Naming things has always been a challenge for me. Take, for instance, the Standard Sock Co (the brand I talk about in the previous chapter that was impossible to find online) or my first design agency, Monocle. As my business partnership with Paul Breen at 6.2 was amicably dissolving in 2016, I was in the throes of establishing what would become Reny. However, this transition didn't happen without a few hiccups.

While notifying a new client of my venture into design and brand building, he inquired about the name of my new business. This was something I hadn't considered yet. Glancing around my studio, my eyes landed on a shelf full of *Monocle* magazines. In a spontaneous moment, I blurted out, 'Monocle'. The client, noting its similarity to the magazine, sparked awkward exchanges and an eventual realisation of my inadvertent naming issues.

*Monocle* magazine was first published in 2007, founded by Tyler Brûlé. As its popularity and potential grew, Brûlé secured a hefty investment from Nikkei Inc., and they began a global audit on the use of the word 'Monocle', extending their trademark to include 'Monocle and Digital'. That's when they discovered my little venture, and I received an unexpected call from their lawyer. I explained the honest coincidence, which led to an understanding response and a grace period to change my business name. What initially sounded like a dire legal threat became a friendly resolution, allowing me three months to transition to a new name.

# INSIGHTS

Years later, I encountered Brûlé at a social event, and I mentioned my business had, for a short time, shared a name with his publication. We had a lighthearted chat about it, and he seemed amused and appreciative of my 'inspired' naming choice.

Brûlé's unconventional approach to business and lifestyle has always struck a chord with me. His work, marked by a commitment to journalistic integrity, a flair for innovative design and a broad global outlook, has carved out a unique niche for *Monocle* in the media world.

Following the conversation with the lawyer about my business name, I took it as an opportunity for a fresh start. The next day, I rebranded my business to Reny, embracing a new chapter while carrying forward the lessons and inspirations from leaders like Brûlé.

Have you seen the movie *Unbreakable*, directed by M. Night Shyamalan? It's intriguing and brilliant at the same time. The story revolves around Elijah Price, or 'Mr Glass', a man with brittle bone syndrome. Price believes that if he is so fragile, there must be someone on the other end of the spectrum whose bones don't break. If someone can be so brittle, why can't someone be unbreakable? This framework for the movie still intrigues me today. If someone was unbreakable, how would we know? I have never broken a bone — am I indestructible? I am not that keen to take the test to find out!

**What if our habits were not set in stone? What if every day was a complete refresh and a new start, with our past shaping nothing about us except our values and choices?**

This brings me back to Pierre Bourdieu and his habitus theory — what if the opposite were true? What if our habits were not set in stone? What if every day was a complete refresh and a new start, with our past shaping nothing about us except our values and choices? That intrigues me. What if, despite all the subconscious conditioning and societal influences, we could wake up each day and choose who we want to be, forging new paths and habits at will? It's a radical idea but one worth exploring.

I think we can do more than simply understand how our environment shapes us. We can challenge the notion that our past binds us. We can reinvent ourselves and make conscious choices that break away from ingrained patterns. While habits are powerful, they are not unchangeable. Creativity and intention can reshape our lives and design our futures.

# INSIGHTS

The concept of the adjacent possible was introduced by Stuart Kauffman, a theoretical biologist and complex systems researcher. He originally proposed the term in the context of evolutionary biology, explaining how biological systems explore nearby possibilities as they evolve. The concept has since been popularised in various fields, including innovation, creativity, and technology. Steven Johnson discussed it extensively in his book Where *Good Ideas Come From: The Natural History of Innovation*, where he applied the idea to innovation and creativity, illustrating how ideas and possibilities emerge by building on what is already possible. He likens the development of ideas and technology to a house that magically expands with each door you open. Each room leads to another set of doors, revealing a new array of previously inaccessible possibilities. This theory suggests that innovation is a step-by-step process, where ideas evolve from their current state to what's immediately adjacent. It emphasises the importance of exploring the boundaries of our current knowledge and understanding, because this is where the potential for innovation lies. Johnson's concept encourages us to look beyond the familiar, embrace the unknown and understand that the future unfolds as a spectrum of possibilities shaped by our explorations and discoveries. His insights inspire us to think about how individuals and societies can navigate and expand our 'adjacent possible' to foster creativity and drive progress.

I firmly believe we are the architects of our destiny, with the innate ability to form new habits, craft fresh stories and unlock new horizons. We can align our daily actions with our deepest aspirations and values, using our creative confidence as the engine for transformation.

Again, we come back to creative confidence, and having the courage to show up, begin and engage. This is in contrast to the often misunderstood concept of innovation—after all, what we commonly refer to as 'innovation' isn't something you can simply decide to do. Innovation is the natural outcome of starting, conversing and actively listening. We can't 'innovate' on demand, but we can create, write, listen, talk and sing. Through these actions, new ideas and solutions spontaneously emerge.

Kauffman's adjacent possible concept means adopting a mindset of exploration and growth. Just as the journey of ideas is a series of expanding possibilities, so is your capacity to shape the future. Each step you take into the unknown reveals new paths and opportunities. This metaphor isn't just an abstract concept; it's a call to action. By actively engaging in your 'adjacent possible', you're not merely contemplating change but driving it, using your creativity, resilience and dialogue to mould a prosperous future with purpose.

Products like the Commodore 64 or the iconic Sony Walkman that Nobutoshi Kihara and his team crafted remind us of thoughtful design's lasting impact. These weren't just products but gateways to new experiences, shaping culture and consumer behaviour for years.

As we stand on the brink of discoveries and creations, it's worth pondering what our contribution will be. Could you design something that will become as iconic as those created in 1985? The idea that everything around us was once just a concept in someone's mind is humbling and exhilarating. The iconic products of the past were designed by individuals who dared to dream and act on their vision.

> **As you navigate your adjacent possible, remember that you're not just designing for today but crafting tomorrow's legacy.**

Now, it's your turn. What will you design? How will you harness the lessons of the past and today's tools to create something that connects you with the future? As you navigate your adjacent possible, remember that you're not just designing for today but crafting tomorrow's legacy. Your creativity, decisions and courage to venture into the unknown will shape the iconic experiences of the next generation. So, take a moment to reflect, and then step forward with confidence and curiosity.

## INSIGHTS

Real breakthroughs come from exploring what's right in front of you and gradually expanding your reach to uncover new possibilities.

Move forward one idea at a time. Push boundaries slowly, allowing creativity to build momentum. Each step brings you closer to something new.

Remember—progress isn't always dramatic. Instead, it's steady, purposeful and transformative.

# PART VI

# HORIZONS: GROWTH

**Where mastery and continuous growth become the horizon, and creativity evolves into an ever-expanding pursuit**

Creativity is a journey; growth is remaining open, curious and adaptable — constantly looking toward new horizons. I've come to see that creative confidence isn't a destination but an ongoing evolution. Each challenge is a chance to refine your ideas and expand your vision. When you embrace growth as a mindset, your creativity knows no bounds, and neither does your confidence.

CHAPTER 16

# TIME AFTER TIME

Understanding that growth in creativity
is a continuous process

In 1990, the air over Kuwait and Iraq was thick with the tension and smoke of Operation Desert Storm, a conflict that captured global attention and headlines. Finally released from prison in February 1990, Nelson Mandela continued his tireless campaign against apartheid, igniting global conversations on freedom and equality. The digital realm would soon mark its revolution by launching the world's first website, setting the stage for the internet age.

Yet, I focused my world on a seemingly more important event — the school dance. While leaders negotiated and armies mobilised, the nerve-wracking prospect of asking Crystal Anshaw for the last dance of the night at the local school disco preoccupied me. During adolescence, the vast dramas of the outside world paled compared to the social rituals of high school life.

As Mandela spoke of freedom, my life revolved around a few heart-pounding minutes on a dance floor. I love this about being young, where teenage social life trials eclipse the realities of global events. Hopefully, this universal rite of passage isn't lost in the new world of constant information, screens and data. Every day should present a new challenge, something new, like being 15 again! I now search for that feeling through my work, this book, design and art.

By 1990, grunge music was building on the horizon, soon to become the soundtrack to my life, dominated by bands such as Nirvana, Pearl Jam, Stone Temple Pilots and Candlebox. I tore my stone-washed Bros jeans at the knee. I grew a mullet like Jason Donavon and started wearing my check button-down shirts open. But I had a problem, a teenage juxtaposition I had never spoken about. It was so profound that it tore me in all kinds of emotional directions and took me years to understand and to share. My real musical obsession was with Cyndi Lauper.

Since her debut album, *She's So Unusual*, dropped in 1983 and her song 'The Goonies 'R' Good Enough' popped up on the soundtrack of one of the greatest films ever made, *The Goonies*, I had fallen in love with her. It was a closet-based love affair, however, one I dared speak of. In a world starting to echo with aggressive grunge chords, my adoration for Cyndi Lauper was my own Desert Storm!

But here is what a song can do — or, more specifically, how it can heighten the profound importance of a moment in time.

It's 10 pm on a Friday in Penrith, 1990. The school dance is in full swing under a cloud of smoke machines and dim lights. In his infinite wisdom, the DJ calls out for the 'Men in the room to grab their girls'. (My kids' disgust of the sexism and chauvinism would overshadow their love of the 1990s). But I hear it as a call to action. I spring into step, ready to grab my girl! I search through the hazy room for Crystal Anshaw. Suddenly, I see her. Of course, she's standing beside me, reaching for my hand, which I take without hesitation as we glide onto the dance floor. I stare into her eyes as I walk backward through the dense crowd of slow dancers; I've grabbed my girl!

Cyndi Lauper's 'Time After Time' is playing, and I am mouthing the words to her as we dance. I'm leading — the room parts for us. Everyone had been waiting for this moment to watch us dance. Everyone! As the smoke clears, a circle forms around us. I break free and start solo dancing... a microphone appears in my hands, and I begin singing. The girls in the room, even the ones 'the men had grabbed', start crying and reaching for me ...

Ahem. It's 10 pm on a Friday in Penrith, 1990. The school dance is in full swing under a cloud of smoke machines and dim lights. In his infinite wisdom, the DJ calls out for the 'Men in the room to grab their girls'. (Yes, that part happened.) I'm scanning the crowded room through the hazy darkness, and Crystal is nowhere in sight. Halfway through the song, with only a sparse crowd shuffling on the dance floor, I find her. Casually, with all the confidence I can muster, I say, 'Hi Crystal, I didn't know you were here. Want to dance?' Crystal nods and says, 'Sure'.

As we awkwardly shuffle onto the dance floor, I'm grappling with a critical decision: hands on hips or shoulders? The ghost of my brother's infamous 'white man's overbite' manoeuvre (from chapter 9) haunts me still. I nervously bite my upper lip and reach out, aiming for hips and shoulders. *Oh Jesus*, I thought. Before I knew it, I'd latched onto her neck! Yes, her neck; my hands are now firmly wrapped around Crystal's neck, and my fingers are intertwined like I'm performing a yoga stretch around it. I sense the same unease from Crystal, her hands flailing in the distant gap between us. She settled for my hips. We shuffle on. Still today, these 45 seconds of neck holding and hip resting lives as the single most awkward moment of my life.

Then relief steps in. Mr Pasqua, our ever-observant maths teacher, comes to our rescue. He guides my hands to a more appropriate position on Crystal's sides and her hands on my shoulders. He looks at us both and says in his American accent, 'Relax, dancing is fun!' We both laugh out loud as the tension breaks. I can hear the music. We dance to 'Time After Time' and the teenage battlefield of awkward glances and nervous laughs fades away for those few minutes. It is just us, the music, my hidden favourite singer of all time and the girl I had 'grabbed' to share it with.

*Disclaimer:* I have never grabbed a girl. Donald Trump's got us covered in that department!

Cyndi Lauper would continue to weave through my life, becoming a personal soundtrack played through earphones or on solitary car rides. Yet, like the awkward steps of a school dance or the tumultuous path of my early business ventures, Lauper's early career echoed similar themes of resilience. Her music mirrored my struggles and rebuilding.

## INSIGHTS

During the late 1970s in New York City, Cyndi Lauper fronted the band Blue Angel, blending rockabilly vibes with the burgeoning new wave scene. This was when the city's streets buzzed with the raw energy of punk, new wave and the developing sounds of hip-hop. Amid this gritty backdrop, female artists such as Patti Smith and Lydia Lunch were carving out their spaces, often pushing back against a music industry favouring men. Despite the vibrant scene, women faced considerable challenges — from overt sexism to restrictive stereotypes that dictated how a female musician should look and sound.

*(continued)*

Blue Angel's journey was symbolic of these challenges. While they exuded undeniable energy onstage, the reality was far grimmer. Financial strains and legal battles soon overwhelmed the band, forcing Lauper into bankruptcy by 1981. This period of struggle was a testament to the harsh realities many women faced in the industry, where systemic barriers often overshadowed their talents.

Yet Lauper's unique voice and eclectic style set her apart. Even in a field crowded with the likes of Debbie Harry and the raucous spirit of punk rockers, her early days with Blue Angel laid the groundwork for her later solo success.

In 1983 Lauper released her first solo album, *She's So Unusual*, which included breakout hits such as 'Girls Just Want to Have Fun' and 'She Bob' (as well as my favourite, 'Time After Time'). 'True Colours', released in 1986 on the album of the same name, became a source of comfort and nostalgia during my mum's battle with cancer, with the song's authenticity and emotional depth speaking to those who felt misunderstood or sidelined.

My daughter Pip is a Cindy Lauper fan, too — although she will hate me for saying that; she is more of a Zach Bryan type these days. (As she gets older, I can *hear* the eyes roll these days without even needing to see it.) Pip has always exuded a sense of confidence and contentment in her own skin. She has sung confidently and passionately in the backseat of the car since she could talk. When Pip was seven, on a drive home, she started singing Cyndi Lauper's version of 'I Drove All Night', belting it out with all her heart. Pip always had an affinity for eighties culture, old movies, neon art and fashion. She forever chips away at her hand-written list of eighties and nineties films.

We share a bond built on conversation, trust and storytelling, and spend many late nights laughing out loud. Her insights into complex films and books are profound; she can break down the most intricate narratives. Pip plays bass guitar and piano and speaks French. She once competed at the Australian National Downhill Ski Titles, placing in the top 10 — and then promptly declared, 'Well, I'm never doing that again!' Despite her natural athletic prowess — she is often the first to be spotted by coaches for her height on basketball courts and grace on the ski slopes — Pip forges her own path.

Pip's bravery isn't like Miff's 70-foot-jump kind; it's rooted in knowing when to stand her ground against injustice and inequality. She's not afraid to lean in and use her voice, which she learned from her mum and grandparents. She is a young woman with a voice and is abundant in creative confidence, which inspires me every day. This is the beauty of having kids and watching them grow, each in their own way. As the self-proclaimed best skier in the family, Pip is fiercely independent and brave, carving out her place in the world.

# INSIGHTS

The late 1970s and early 1980s marked the beginning of a significant shift in music as women like Cyndi Lauper began taking their rightful place at the forefront of the industry. But she had to claw her way back first.

I know bankrupts who give up on their dreams; they fail and stop. In Australia, people are terrified of bankruptcy; it has a stigma of the ultimate failure. 'How dare someone dream so hard and not make something work?' people seem to wonder. I think of it differently. I think bankruptcy protects the dreamers, believers and brave ones who have enough courage to chase something bigger than themselves. If you have a dream, chase it. Perhaps it does work, the business goes broke, and you go bankrupt. Start again; that lesson and the knowledge will be the foundation for something extraordinary—better, more innovative, closer to perfect. I know this to be true. Don't let the end be the end; let it be a new beginning.

The failure of Blue Angel was a new beginning for Cyndi Lauper. She worked in supermarkets and cafes to reset and start again while chasing gigs in the New York clubs.

Then, one night, in the evening glow of her room and with the hustle and bustle of New York City as her backdrop, she put pen to paper. She wrote a song that would find its way from her living room to yours, from her pen and paper to that night in Penrith with Crystal, to the quiet moments alone with my thoughts, to be used as a sign of strength for my mum's fight with cancer. Words written at one place became inspiration and strength for someone else because she was brave enough to keep going.

In 1983, fate would step in for Cyndi, like it does for anyone daring to dream, when manager David Wolff saw her unique

*(continued)*

mix of vulnerability and vitality—offering a contract, validation and belief. The 1983 release of *She's So Unusual* propelled her into the limelight, making her songs anthems of individuality and strength.

All creative odysseys begin somewhere. Sometimes, they begin in solitude, in an apartment in New York. Other times, they begin in a crowd, most often from the margins, where we feel disenchantment, loss or pain.

A single thread connects creativity with ideas: courage. Courage means diving into the unknown and trusting your unique perspective and voice. The boldness to express yourself authentically, without guarantees of reception or acclaim, embodies the purest form of creativity.

I often hear people say, 'I used to draw, build, or create. But I'm not creative anymore.' This notion assumes that creativity is a static trait confined to the past. It's a flawed perspective that disregards a crucial reality: creativity isn't about who you were or what you made then. It's about who you decide to be or what you decide to make tomorrow.

The belief that creativity is some innate talent that fades with time or is shackled to the past is a myth. This view neglects the essential nature of creativity: it's a deliberate act, a continuous series of decisions and actions that shape your identity and chart your future.

Life is full of unexpected twists and lessons that compel us to reconsider and adapt. These moments demand flexibility, urging us to rethink our course and embrace changes that might once have seemed daunting. These pivot points are where our creativity is tested—and where our potential for growth lies.

At work, I often talk about sunk costs, a concept first introduced by Seth Godin that has given me a lot of confidence. This idea has helped me navigate the many mistakes I've made in business, allowing me to pause, accept that I messed up, and move on.

'Sunk costs' refer to past investments in time, money or emotion. These 'investments' — and not wanting to walk away from them — can lock us into a future that's no longer right for us. This idea challenges us to examine what we've poured our resources into and accept that just because we've invested a lot doesn't mean we should keep throwing good after bad.

Take my and Nicola's experience with Standard Sock Co, for example, which I talk about in chapter 14. We invested $150 000 into launching this brand, including production, stock, website, branding and marketing costs. We believed in the product and its potential, but we hit an unforeseen obstacle — the name 'Standard Sock Co' was lost in the vast expanse of the internet. No matter what we did, the name didn't gain traction online.

Imagine — we had invested all that money and effort and now, facing this branding dilemma, we had to decide whether to invest even more to turn things around. The initial $150 000 were our sunk costs, meaning they shouldn't influence future decisions. What mattered was whether additional investment would solve the problem or cutting our losses and pivoting was better.

We had to consider the option to stop investing in Standard Sock Co and instead direct our resources towards a new venture with a more distinctive name and better market potential. The decision boiled down to what would likely bring the most value and align with our goals: trying to salvage a struggling brand, or pursuing a new opportunity for better prospects.

We had already spent the money on Standard Sock Co, and continuing just because we'd invested so much made little sense. So we focused on looking forward and deciding based on future benefits rather than justifying past choices. While we wish we could, we can't be everywhere all at once, so we reset our focus and handed Standard Sock Co to Steve Fisher from Sportfactor.

Breaking free from the sunk cost mindset means making choices based on what's ahead, not what's behind. It's about making decisions that look to the future benefits instead of trying to justify past choices. And keep in mind I'm not just talking about invested money here — it applies to jobs, relationships and personal goals. Staying in a career you hate because you have invested time into is an injustice to yourself, the legacy you create and the future you have yet to live.

> **Breaking free from the sunk cost mindset means making choices based on what's ahead, not what's behind.**

When you understand this, knowing when to keep going and when it's wiser to change course becomes easier. This understanding helps us live smarter.

# INSIGHTS

Being overly attached to past decisions and past journeys is part of the broader narrative of innovation and creativity. 'Done is better than perfect', reminds us that the quest for perfection can sometimes hinder progress. In pursuing perfection, we risk losing the importance of completion—the act of moving forward and evolving.

This concept holds profound implications for design, business and personal growth. The idea isn't about the initial creative spark but the ability and courage to adapt and pivot when the situation demands. This approach acknowledges that change is an inevitable—and necessary—part of growth. You need both the foresight to recognise when a change in direction is needed and the courage to embrace it.

Your path is not linear but a winding road marked by persistence and readiness. In adopting this mindset, you open yourself up to a world of possibilities, where each decision, whether to continue or pivot, brings you closer to realising potential.

This underscores a fundamental truth: creativity isn't just about innovating or crafting something new. It's about being present, having the courage to start somewhere, and the willingness to embark on a journey. Putting pen to paper, brush to canvas, mind to the problem, or even sharing a simple smile are the seeds of significant change and impact.

**Creativity is an innate power within us all. It's the courage to express and materialise our thoughts, emotions and visions, whatever the medium.**

Creativity is an innate power within us all. It's the courage to express and materialise our thoughts, emotions and visions, whatever the medium.

Creativity isn't confined to grand gestures or revolutionary ideas in a world that often measures success through innovation and tangible achievements. It's found in quiet moments of reflection, minor acts of kindness, or the bravery to share our narratives and experiences. We connect with ourselves and others in these moments, igniting transformation and inspiring growth.

# INSIGHTS

Creative confidence isn't a burst of inspiration—it's about persistence, patience and the act of showing up again and again. Setbacks aren't failures; they're signals to help you adjust, refine and grow.

Take the long view. Creativity unfolds over time, shaped by your commitment and your willingness to evolve. Every step, no matter how small, adds to your creative confidence.

Let time be your ally, allowing your work to deepen and your vision to take shape.

# CHAPTER 17

# WHY SO SIRIUS?!

Exploring creative mastery without losing sight of joy and curiosity

It's March, and I'm sitting on a balcony of architect Harry Seidler's very own apartment, the Seidler Penthouse in North Sydney. The weather is warm, and the sun is setting over the harbour. Courtney van der Weyden from the Powerhouse Museum is sitting beside me. Courtney and I had been working together for about five years and she remains one of my favourite humans. We were there to watch my friend Tim Ross and his best mate Kit Warhurst perform their stand-up show, 'Man About the House'. We arrived early by taxi and joined Tim on the balcony for a beer as he prepared for the show.

Tim Ross, also known as 'Rosso', is an Australian comedian, radio host and television presenter known for his humour and charisma. He gained fame as part of the comedy duo 'Merrick and Rosso' with Merrick Watts, and the pair became well known for their radio show on Triple J and, later, Nova 96.9. Besides his comedy work, Tim has also become involved in architecture and design. He created the popular show *Streets of Your Town*, which explored modernist architecture and its cultural significance in Australia. Tim is passionate about design and has advocated for preserving architectural landmarks. His work bridges entertainment and cultural advocacy, emphasising the importance of architectural heritage and community spaces.

Sitting on the Seidler Penthouse balcony, Tim looked effortlessly cool. His hair was wavy, his beard immaculately groomed. He was wearing a scarf and a denim shirt with the top five buttons open. The scarf was one of those scarves that was more about fashion and less about function. It looked fabulous. I wanted one. Tim is one of those friends who keeps getting better with age; every time we catch up, he looks better. Most of my friends are like me — facing hair loss, some extra weight and creaky knees. Tim is a real-life version of Benjamin Button. Over the years, our regular catch-ups have become a cherished tradition. Tim always settles into a corner chair, crosses his legs and leans back, fully engaged and genuinely interested in our conversations. He's a provocateur of great conversation, not just talking but listening intently.

Like Tim, I also love architecture. As I get older, I become more and more obsessed with it. In my next life, I want to become an architect, designing buildings and reshaping our cities. But that's not me, not right now. And back on the balcony, I'm having a beer with Tim and he looks relaxed. The penthouse overlooks Sydney's Luna Park, a classic venue, and I feel almost famous. Okay, not famous; just 'pretend famous' by association.

Tim is about to do a show he has been working on for a long time, tailored to various locations. He brings people into modernist, architecturally designed homes by famous architects, homes often inaccessible to ordinary folks like us. He lets them wander through the rooms and then shares Australian stories about the places — how they came to be, the stories they hold and the lives they shaped. Today, these shows remain my favourite to attend in Australia.

# INSIGHTS

Tim Ross is a vibrant embodiment of creativity on a unique journey, transitioning from a beloved comedian to a pivotal voice in architecture and design. Our paths first crossed two decades ago when Tim visited my office in Surry Hills with an old friend of mine. This initial meeting sparked a friendship that has flourished over the years, marked by mutual support and a shared passion for creative expression, the arts and good conversation.

One evening in 2013, at the Observer Hotel in The Rocks, Sydney, I shared a drink with Tim. This wasn't just a casual meet-up, but a critical moment of reflection. Already celebrated for his comedic genius and distinctive voice on radio, Tim was at a crossroads, eager to pivot towards his passion for architecture and design.

That night, Tim delved into discussions about the future; I was struck by Tim's unwavering dedication to effecting change beyond the laughter. It marked the beginning of his journey from being known as 'Rosso', the comedian, to becoming a respected advocate in the architectural and design world, spearheading unwavering efforts to preserve our modernist heritage and bring pivotal Australian stories of design back to life.

He wrote and hosted critically acclaimed documentaries such as *Streets of Your Town* and, more recently, *Designing a Legacy*, using his platform to spotlight architectural icons and the stories that inhabit them. His leadership played a crucial role in the campaign to save the Sirius building, illustrating his shift from humour to cultural commentary, yet always maintaining his charm and wit.

The Sirius building in Sydney is a significant example of Brutalist architecture, designed by Tao Gofers and completed in 1980. Originally built to provide public housing, it became iconic for its unique design and prime location overlooking Sydney Harbour. The structure features robust concrete forms and modular units, characteristic of Brutalist design and aimed at addressing the urban housing crisis of its time. The building's historical and architectural value came under threat when plans for its demolition emerged, sparking public outcry. Tim, among others, led a vigorous campaign to preserve Sirius, emphasising its cultural and social importance. The campaign highlighted the building's role in providing affordable housing and its place in Sydney's architectural landscape. Their efforts aimed to protect the building from redevelopment and ensure its legacy as a symbol of accessible urban living and architectural innovation.

Tim's talks, often held in historically significant homes across Australia (and some overseas locations), are not mere lectures but vibrant narratives that breathe life into the walls of these modernist treasures. I've had the honour of participating in these events, from managing the bar at the bank in Port Kembla to assisting at the door at the iconic Rose Seidler House in Wahroonga. Each event is a testament to Tim's ability to draw people into the nuanced folds of architecture and design, making the past relevant and exhilarating for today's audience.

My mum admired Tim immensely, and was especially fond of Tim and Michelle's kids, Bugsy and Bobby. Tim was an amazing support for me during my mum's battle with cancer. He consistently inquired about her wellbeing and fondly brought her up long after passing, and these constant check-ins were a great comfort. His nurturing presence during those challenging times exemplified the genuine care and connection he fosters within his community and amongst friends.

Mum particularly liked Tim's series, *Streets of Your Town*, where he addressed the changing dynamics of architecture and its impact on community connections. He discussed how modern architecture often misses the vital element of community engagement. Unlike the days of old when arriving home meant opening up to neighbourhood interactions — for example, waving to a neighbour or chatting in the driveway — modern designs encourage a more isolated existence with their remote-controlled garages and private entries. My mum would talk about that episode a lot, wondering why people entered the garage and then entered the house from the garage, bypassing an important wave to the neighbours.

My mum cherished the traditional Australian community spirit, where neighbourly connections were central to daily life. Tim's work rekindles appreciation of these communal aspects, celebrating the architectural designs that foster community engagement and reminding us of the value of shared spaces and casual interactions that strengthen communal bonds.

Back at the Seidler Penthouse in North Sydney, Courtney and I settled into the back of the room, ready for an evening of laughter and design. Tim's comedy always hits the mark with me, and his yarns and casual storytelling always bring me to tears.

That night, Tim and Kit didn't disappoint as, in a room of young and old, people leaned in, listening, laughing, smiling and connecting. What a gift the arts bring to people's lives.

Jump forward to the start of 2024, and my wife and I attended a business meeting for B Corp in Sydney. I met an architect there and, on meeting, as I often do, mentioned my relationship with Tim as a standard connection. He responded that no-one has done more for architecture and preserving the stories and places we create in this country than Tim.

I think back to that beer in The Rocks in 2013, when Tim was suffering from a crisis in creative confidence and his concern about change. But he woke up the next day, rolled up his sleeves, purchased a fabulous scarf with zero technical value and transformed himself into an icon of Australian design, architecture and, I think, connection!

◊◊◊

I love these stories about finding creative confidence so much; they inspire us, of course, but they do so much more than that — they tell us that we can find our confidence, too. Let me give you another example. My sister-in-law, Clare Hogarth, is one of my dearest friends. We have known each other half of our lives and, of course, share a common connection — that being a love of the same family. My mother-in-law, Lorraine, and father-in-law, Peter, have been the backbone of Clare and Nicola's youth and my adulthood, constantly guiding and supporting us through the challenges life throws at us. Clare's kids, of course, are now adults, Jack and Emily. I love them like they were my own.

When I met Clare in England in 1998, she was a young mum, having had her first son, Jack, at 22 (super young by today's standards!), and her second, Emily, at 25. Clare worked full-time, with two kids, and lived in a small house in Bristol. In October 2005, Clare, her husband, Dave, and their young family decided to do what many people can't imagine: they packed up everything and moved their whole family across the world to settle in Sydney and be closer to Nicola.

Clare wasn't escaping Bristol; Clare and Dave (the brother I wished I had growing up) were enriching their family's life experience and broadening their horizons. The move to Sydney was a proactive step towards creating a nurturing environment for Jack and Emily, surrounded by the love and support of extended family.

Clare immersed herself in the vibrant local culture and natural beauty of Sydney. I recall participating in numerous fun runs together, but one moment stood out. One morning at Shelly Beach in Manly, she wanted to join me for an ocean swim. Clare had never swum in the ocean before (except wading in the waves). At the time, I was ocean swimming weekly, often racing on weekends and doing two-kilometre swims a few mornings each week. I was obsessed — but, please, don't confuse obsession with talent. I was crap.

I remember competing in the Cole Classic ocean swim event, and qualifying for the finals. The finals took place at Manly, starting from Shelly Beach with a two-kilometre swim to Manly Beach, with the event at the time sponsored by *Men's Health* magazine. On making the finals of the event, I felt insecure about my appearance. Wanting to look my best for any potential *Men's Health* photographers, I boosted myself with some self-tanning cream. Two coats later, I looked like a bronzed god, ready to take on the world.

I finished the race mid-field and strutted up the beach, feeling like a million bucks. Right at the finish line, I spotted my old mate Kieran Gilbert (nicknamed Giblet), now chief political reporter for Sky News, standing with his microphone and camera crew. He saw me and said, 'Rennie, let's do a quick interview!' Perfect timing — I was tanned, fit and in my speedos, and my goggles were strapped to my forehead. Despite all my achievements, this felt like the most hilariously insignificant reason of my life for an interview on national TV. Nonetheless, I was all in.

I puffed out my chest and gave Giblet, a former fast bowler who I'd travelled with to the Northern Territory with the U/16 NSW cricket team, a hearty man hug as he prepared me for the interview, surrounded by thousands of beach revellers and the bright lights of the camera. Giblet and I had a history, also playing together in the NSW U/19 team with Stuart Clark and Brett Lee. This was going to be fun.

As I started talking about the gruelling conditions, Giblet listened intently, nodding along. But then, something changed. He glanced down at my body with a look of horror. Not a casual glance — this was a full-on, 'What the hell is that?' stare. I sensed his awkwardness and paused. Giblet gestured for me to look down. *Wait, was it my Speedos?* I thought Was something loose amid the concealment of the world's smallest swimmers, a ball perhaps? 'Don't look', I said to myself, 'keep talking, rise above it'. I kept talking until he interrupted. 'Rennie, seriously mate, there's something wrong down there. What's going on?'

I looked down and, to my horror, saw that my legs looked similar to those of a wild zebra. The self-tanning lotion had streaked through the swim, leaving me with ridiculous stripes up and down my legs and torso. Giblet, trying to keep a straight face, said, 'Rennie, you need to get that shit checked out'. I laughed nervously, 'Yeah, what is that? Oh, gawd', as I awkwardly tried to hug him again. He backed off, chuckling. 'Seriously, mate, go and get that fixed. That ain't good.' I quickly grabbed a towel and made a hasty exit, leaving a trail of laughter and confusion.

Back to Clare, who (despite my self-tanning debacle) had recently taken an interest in my ocean swimming. On that warm October morning at Shelly Beach, she decided to join me for a swim to Manly Beach while the rest of the family walked the coastal path. With its golden sands and crystal-clear waters, Shelly Beach was bustling with early morning activity. Clare, who had never swum in the ocean, faced the challenge head-on. Her first ocean swim was a blend of trepidation and triumph.

As we stretched across the bay, Clare initially looked comfortable, entirely at ease in the ocean — until she wasn't. As we got further from the shore, Clare kept asking me questions — what was beneath us, and what if we couldn't make it back to the shore? Her goggles added to the anxiety as sea life continued to swim underneath us. Halfway through the roughly one-kilometre swim, Clare grabbed my arm in a slight panic, overwhelmed by the ocean's vastness. Then she grabbed my other arm. Now, my qualifying for the Cole Classic finals aside, swimming with no arms is hard and, at that moment, I had a terrifying thought: *Is this it for me, drowned at sea by my sister-in-law?*

Pushing aside that thought, I aimed for calm. 'Lay on your back, Clare,' I said. 'Just float and look at the sky. Don't swim, just float. We can do this all day — float. We don't even need to swim.' That was enough to calm the nerves. No-one ever gave me any credit for saving my life that day, but that's okay. It's a tick in the box — saved my own life.

We pushed on, and I saw Clare's stroke gain momentum as we approached the shore. Usually, most people feel tired towards the end — not Clare. She gained momentum and lifted. It was a metaphor for how she lives her life, rising when things get hard.

As we finally reached the shore, Clare was beaming, a mix of exhaustion and exhilaration on her face. 'That was incredible!' she exclaimed. 'I never thought I could do it.'

I couldn't help but smile, feeling almost like a drowned rat. 'Yeah, you did it!'

What began as a tentative wade into the waters soon became a decisive moment of self-discovery and empowerment. This wasn't just a swim; it was Clare's bold declaration of her willingness to embrace the unknown and her ability to rise above it — or, more accurately, above anything.

Shortly after that swim, Clare revisited her childhood love of bike riding. This time, Clare and the family visited us when we were living in Melbourne. We lived in Brighton right on the bay, and I used to ride my old Orbea road bike to work every day. It was a simple 15-kilometre ride along Port Phillip Bay into Port Melbourne. Clare was intrigued and, over coffee one morning, explained she hadn't ridden a bike since she was 13.

Fascinated, we went outside for a roll on my road bike. The high seat and thin wheels were a challenge, so we lowered the seat and Clare, determined, wobbled up the road on my bike. Reminiscent of that morning at Shelly Beach, she found a way to ride. At first, watching her turn corners was like watching a Mack truck do a three-point turn, but she rode on, determined to work it out.

The experience was exhilarating for Clare, reawakening her sense of adventure and freedom. That same day, Clare and Dave headed into Melbourne, and she purchased a new road bike — not a casual one with a basket, but a sleek race bike designed for high speeds. She was hooked.

Four weeks later, Clare called me to join her in the Nepean Triathlon. This transformation was not only physical, but also deeply personal. I vividly recall a conversation with her at the Glenbrook Hotel the night before the triathlon. With a steely yet thoughtful gaze, she shared her realisation that, while she had been a dedicated and wonderful mother, it was time to embrace a new chapter. She wanted to lead by example, showing that she could be a nurturing parent who also pursues their dreams with relentless dedication. This wasn't just about self-improvement; it was also about setting an example for Jack and Emily, showing them that life is about balance, courage and pursuing your goals.

Clare's next challenge was an Ironman event — one of the most challenging endurance races in the world. It consists of a 3.9-kilometre swim, a 180-kilometre bike ride and a 42.2-kilometre marathon. Completing one requires extraordinary physical and mental stamina, as athletes must endure harsh conditions, gruelling terrain and extreme fatigue.

Just 18 months before her first Ironman (Ironwoman) in Port Macquarie, New South Wales, Clare hadn't sat on a bike since she was 13, had never swum in the ocean, and had only recently taken up running. Her journey from that anxiety-filled ocean swim where she almost drowned us both to completing not one but two Ironman events is nothing short of remarkable. Clare's determination and rapid transformation highlight her incredible resilience and strength, proving that even the loftiest goals are achievable with unwavering commitment and courage.

## INSIGHTS

When we met, Clare was a secretary working for her dad. Today, she is a leader of a global brand. Clare's journey from her tranquil life in Bristol to the adrenaline-fueled world of Ironman competitions and the boardrooms of international leadership is a narrative of courage, transformation and the enduring power of the human spirit.

Her story inspires everyone who hears it. It reminds us that we are not defined by the roles we play, but by the choices we make and the challenges we dare to face.

Sometimes, all it takes is the courage to swim when you think you can't, to get back on the bike despite the wobbles, or to run by just putting one foot in front of the other.

I don't know if Tim and Clare have ever met, but writing about this makes me think they would be good buddies, too. I've seen Rosso speak publicly at least 20 times now. He tells remarkable stories about living in his beautiful part of Sydney and, as a rad Aussie celebrity, he lives next door to many famous people.

One of his famous neighbours was renowned Australian singer and actress Delta Goodrem. At the time, Delta was dating Irish singer Brian McFadden, former member of the boy band Westlife. This pair attracted much media attention, with photographers frequently camped outside Delta's home.

Rosso, always one for a good laugh, saw an opportunity in this constant media presence. He lives in a beautiful old modernist home with a striking glass front, making his daily activities somewhat public. He humorously recalls trying to get the media to take photos of him instead of Delta and Brian. One day, in a bid for attention, he walked down his driveway in his underwear, wheeling out the bins. He jokingly called out to the photographers, 'Hey guys, look at this! It's me, Rosso, in my underwear. Perfect time for a shot!'

One media personnel responded, 'That's the problem with you, Rosso — too much front and not enough substance'. Everyone laughed at his quip.

While Rosso tells this story as a funny anecdote, it reveals to me something deeper about his character. He showcases the humour, yes, but he's also able to dream big and think creatively. The very 'front' that the media referenced gives people like Rosso the courage to stand out, be bold and transform into various roles, much like Clark Kent into Superman.

# INSIGHTS

These stories teach us a fundamental lesson; if you have made it this far in book, this could be the most important lesson you can learn regarding creativity. It is so important that I am writing it in bold and underlining it, much to the frustration of my editor:

## **<u>Creativity is the art of finding a new route to a known destination.</u>**

That feels good reading—and it should be, because it is so simple. Even when you know where you are going, sometimes the road takes time; sometimes, it's windier than anticipated. Do you take the high road, the low road, the ocean view? Your route can be as big as your dream or as simple as you want. Creativity is about synthesising stories into new worlds with endless possibilities. Curiosity fuels creativity. The more curious you are, the more you experience and learn. The more you learn, the more connections your brain makes, leading to unique solutions and perspectives.

When I started writing this book, its working title was *How to Save the World from the Shower!* How many of your best ideas happen in the shower or while watching a movie? Our brains process vast amounts of information, often making unexpected connections in these 'downtimes'.

As I've highlighted throughout this book, we often sell ourselves short, thinking creativity is reserved for those who write plays or create art. But being creative is about doing something human, generous and sometimes risky. It's about solving interesting problems, whether you're an accountant, politician, housekeeper or engineer.

Recognising creativity as a skill is half the battle. We're not born with it; we learn and develop it through practice. Just like lifting heavy objects was once a job, now our job is to show up and solve interesting problems. This requires commitment and practice.

**Solving problems isn't a miracle; it's a skill. Commitment to the process and practice comes before success.**

Solving problems isn't a miracle; it's a skill. Commitment to the process and practice comes before success. You don't wait for miracles to get serious; you practise, and then things start to look effortless.

Seth Godin discusses art not in the traditional sense but as a generous, risky human act intended to create change and connection. Making art involves choosing to do something meaningful over maintaining the status quo. Ultimately, we have to decide if we want to make art — and commit to what it requires.

**Creativity is finding a new route to a known destination.**

What are your chances of doing something for me right now before we move on?

Grab a pen and a pad, the closest one you can find. Write this down and underline it: Creativity is finding a new route to a known destination.

Then write answers to the following questions:

- What is your art?
- Where are you going with your art?

Then write your responses again but a little differently: Creativity is me doing *[first response]* heading towards *[second response]*.

The best part of that exercise is that you didn't have to strip down to your underwear to solve the problem, although I wrote this in my underwear! (Did I? You will never know. But, yes, I am writing this in my underwear.)

## INSIGHTS

I found my creative confidence when I stopped taking life so seriously.

I now know creativity thrives when your approach is both playful and serious. Keep the process lighthearted, letting curiosity and a sense of humour guide you. Balancing mastery with childlike wonder allows your work to be more authentic and meaningful.

Don't let the pursuit of perfection smother your sense of fun. Whether you're telling a story, designing something new or solving a problem, remember to bring joy into the process.

The best solutions come from your curiosity and playfulness.

# CHAPTER 18

# EATEN BY A WHALE

Realising that the creative journey never truly
ends—it's always evolving

In January 1994, I flew to Melbourne to play cricket for the NSW under-19 team. It was my second year on the squad, and we had some strong players, including a young fast bowler from the NSW south coast who had just turned 17 in November of the previous year. His name was Brett Lee. As a second-year player and captain of the NSW City U/19 team, I was asked to mentor Brett—to keep an eye on him and be a role model.

We were seated on the plane, with me in the aisle seat and Brett on my left. Shortly after take-off, we talked about Allan Donald, a South African bowler, who was bowling at speeds of 142 kilometres per hour, at the time the fastest on earth. I asked Brett how fast he wanted to bowl 'when he grew up'. Without blinking, he said, 'Faster than anyone has ever bowled before. Faster than the fastest of all time'. His conviction was unmistakable. Brett would achieve that dream, with his fastest ball clocking a 161.1 kilometres per hour ball against New Zealand in 2005 and becoming one of the fastest bowlers in cricket history. (Only the Pakistani bowler Shoaib Akhtar has bowled faster, as 161.3 kilometres per hour.)

As Brett became a cricket legend, I was on a different path—a path reminiscent of our third night in Melbourne back in 1994 when the team went out for dinner. Afterwards, a few of us—including Garry Sheen, Matt Nicholson, Ash Shoebridge, Shane Deitz, Brett Lee and Cory Richards—went on to a pub with an 11 pm curfew. Everyone else left as the pub turned into a nightclub, but I chose to stay.

I remember dancing all night, blissfully forgetting all about the visions of my brother's 'white man's overbite' that had held me back in the past. At around 1 am, Garry and Matt returned to find me. They walked in and saw me on stage, my NSW polo shirt wrapped around my head like a bandana as I danced barefoot with sweatbands on my wrists. No-one knew where the sweatbands came from, and my shoes were never found again. Reflecting on those days now, with Brett tucked up in bed dreaming of bowling 160 kilometres per hour and me out until 1 am, it seems obvious like our paths were heading in different directions. Our coach, David Moore, who would eventually coach the West Indies Test team, probably refined his judgement of mature role models over the years, but we remain friends to this day. The next day, I scored 55 against Tasmania but was runout while going for a third run, dry heaving while trying to reach the crease.

People often ask me why I never 'made it' in cricket. It's a strange question, one that assumes that 'making it' means being paid or going pro. When I was young, making it meant playing test cricket for Australia — being one of 11 guys out of 200 000. That seemed hard. But I played with and against many who did make it — including Ricky Ponting, Andrew Symonds, Brett Lee and Mike Hussey. It took me a long time to realise my discomfort was because the question was wrong. We're obsessed with the end, forgetting the journey and the moments in between.

I often get asked a similar question relating to my daughter Miff. She's a professional skier and, by the age of 17, she had represented Australia in over 30 events, including multiple World Cups, a Youth Olympic Games, Junior Worlds and an Open World Championship, as she worked towards her qualification for the Olympics at 18. Unfortunately, as I talk about in chapter 13, she suffered a knee injury and missed out on competing in the Olympics. However, she did end up working as a commentator for Channel 7. So, did she make it? She is still making it, and making it never ends.

> **'Making it' is a construct often made up by people who feel they haven't. There's only the present, only the journey.**

The creative journey never ends; the question of whether someone has 'made it' is wrong and, in fact, dangerous. It suggests more about the questioner's state of mind than the person they are asking it about. 'Making it' is a construct often made up by people who feel they haven't. There's only the present, only the journey. When people ask me about Miff, I think of her life in the snow. It's like a dream: filming in Japan and training camps in Italy, California, Utah, Switzerland and New Zealand. Oh, to me, she's made it. But in Miff's world, she's making it happen every day, chasing the thing she dreamed of chasing when she was 10. For me, making it is doing or finding a way to do what you dreamed about, irrespective of the result.

We often discuss this with Miff, along with the idea that Miff is not 'Miff the skier' but 'Miff who skis'. We are not defined by what we do; the end goal does not determine our success. We're defined by how we feel along the way, the moments we collect and the experiences we share. It was difficult when Miff injured her knee, causing her to miss the 2022 Winter Olympic Games. She was down, heartbroken and shattered at 17, watching her peers from the couch (or, eventually, from the Channel 7 studio). Nicola was incredibly supportive during this time, providing Miff a platform to express herself and her emotions. When I was young and struggling with something, I was told to 'look on the bright side', 'suck it up', 'stay positive' and 'everything happens for a reason'. That's bullshit; sometimes, we just need to be told it is okay to feel like shit. It is okay to be sad or scared, and it is okay to be anxious.

It took me a long time to learn that urging people to be positive doesn't boost their resilience in challenging times; it denies their reality. People in pain don't need only good vibes; they need a hand to stay steady through all the emotions. Strength doesn't come from forced smiles; it comes from feeling supported. So that's what we now do in our family.

## INSIGHTS

Some adults think it is okay to ask a teenager what they will do if they don't 'make it' with their chosen dream. To me, this tells the young person one thing: you're not good enough. And it makes the adult an unknowing dickhead.

Similarly, the 'sandwich format' for feedback also comes with challenges. Perhaps you know of, or use, this feedback format. The top of the sandwich says something like, 'That was great, Ben; you look perfect'. The middle of the sandwich is a big 'but you could try doing this, and it will help'. And then the bottom of the sandwich is something like, 'But you look great'. Receiving this sort of feedback as a 15 year old, all I ever heard was some

*(continued)*

overweight hobby coach telling me I was a terrible human who lacked talent. As author and professor Adam Grant highlights, this kind of feedback leads to two distinctive issues:

1. *Positive feedback is often overlooked.* When people receive praise during a feedback conversation, they anticipate criticism. This anticipation can make the initial compliment seem insincere, as if it's only meant to lessen the impact of the forthcoming negative feedback.

2. *If you genuinely focus on the positives, they can overshadow the negatives.* Research indicates that the first and last things said in a conversation are often remembered the most, while the middle is overlooked. When you start and end with positive feedback, the criticism can be overshadowed or disregarded, especially when dealing with a narcissist.

Giving a compliment sandwich might make the giver feel good, but it often doesn't help the receiver. There is a better way.

Of course, there's a difference between welcoming unpleasant emotions and wielding them as weapons. If you haven't read the article 'Chicken Littles are Ruining America', published in *The Atlantic*, google it and do so; it's a powerful reminder that spreading doom and gloom is a self-fulfilling prophecy. No-one needs constant positivity, but everyone does need a sense of possibility.

I didn't want this book to be all positive. Toxic positivity is dangerous. We need to feel present and understand the journey — where we are now and why, and where we want to go and how.

I tell my failure stories with as much pride as my success stories. Sure, in my life, nothing has made me prouder than being a dad to Pip, Kai and Miff. Nothing comes close to how they make me feel. The time I spend with them is more important than any other time I could ever spend. It drives me to create for them, and give them the space to be present. For many years, I underestimated my powers, my true potential.

In 2020, I got my first tattoo on my right hand above my thumb. In this unmissable place, you can't not see it. It says *ikigai*.

*Ikigai* is a Japanese term that blends two words: '*iki*', meaning 'to live', and '*gai*', meaning 'effect, result or use'. Together, the word translates to 'a reason to live'. It's a concept that encourages people to discover what truly matters to them and live a purposeful life. I designed the font myself and had it inked in traditional Japanese. Every time I shake someone's hand, the tattoo reminds me to be present, to think of my value, to ask for my worth and to ensure my work aligns with what the world needs. This tattoo, and the process it encourages, has changed my life. I no longer doubt my value in the world. This helps me be generous and focus on language, my opinions and how I speak to others.

◊◊◊

Raising kids is hard; hands down, it's the hardest thing I have ever done. It always strikes me as interesting that mums who can raise kids stall at believing they can raise a business. My goal as a parent was simple: I wanted to raise generous kids. The way to raise generous kids is to be generous. Teaching kids kindness prepares them for success.

In Italy, studies have shown that the eighth graders with the best grades aren't the ones who got the highest marks five years earlier but the ones who were rated as most helpful. In the United States, middle schoolers who believe their parents value kindness get better grades than those who think their parents put academic and career success first. In Canada, boys who are rated as helpful in kindergarten go on to earn more money in their thirties. Focusing on concern for others leads to a stronger sense of purpose, deeper learning and more prosperous relationships. As a result, it is the fuel for achievement, boosting happiness.

I've always been curious about how to nurture generosity. One of my favourite findings is that nouns are often more effective than verbs. When we shift from 'thank you for helping', for example, to 'thank you for being a helper', kids are more likely to internalise giving as part of their identities.

I've also learned that First Nations Australians often talk about fire differently from non-Indigenous Australians. When I was young and around any sort of fire, my mum would shout, 'Stay away from the fire; you're going to get burned!' However, many Aboriginal and Torres Strait Islander peoples raise their young to understand fire, respect its power and appreciate its role in society and on Country. Young people in these communities learn to use fire as a tool to build community, recognising its importance in cultural practices, land management and sustainability.

The language we use can empower our young people, with even a tiny twist in our words helping them to believe anything is possible. We remember this when our 14 year old decides to take on a 60-foot jump at the Junior World Championships against 19 year olds, believing they can win. Or when our 15 year old shows up for a basketball trial for the NBL's Illawarra Hawks U18 team, just six weeks after picking up the sport — and they make the team. Instead of asking, 'Are you sure you're ready?' we say, 'What a great learning experience this will be'. Or, simply, 'I love to watch you play!' Instead of fearing the worst, we ask, 'What possibilities could come from this?' This shift in perspective helps our kids see opportunities and build confidence in their choices.

By focusing on who they are rather than just what they do, we help young people (and older people... oh, and middle-aged people) see generosity as a core part of themselves. This simple shift in language can significantly impact how they perceive themselves and their actions.

Some of my peers see my junior cricket career as 'wasted talent'. I've heard comments like this a lot and, of course, we hear them all the time about other people: 'He could have made it'; 'She could have been anything'. I can't tolerate these sorts of comments when I hear them. They're based on sweeping assumptions, connecting success with fame and outcomes. We are obsessed with success, yet few of us fully understand it, which is why so many of us don't even start to chase the thing we always dreamed of. We're scared of what people might think; we're afraid we might fail — in terms of the public view of failure. What if we don't make it?

> **Many people accumulate information. Far fewer use it to evolve and improve. The ultimate test of growth is closing the gap between awareness and action.**

I think about my junior cricket life and see it as a treasure of exploration, a beautiful montage of youthful experimentation that taught me bravery — to lean in when it matters and to walk away when it doesn't. The learning process isn't finished when you acquire knowledge. It's complete when you consistently apply that knowledge. Many people accumulate information. Far fewer use it to evolve and improve. The ultimate test of growth is closing the gap between awareness and action.

Progress is about more than just getting better. Sometimes, it's about bouncing back. Success is measured not only by the peaks you reach but also by the valleys you conquer.

Every experience of enduring adversity and overcoming obstacles is a meaningful accomplishment. Resilience is a form of growth.

Again, the path to anywhere is a squiggly line, not a straight one. Instead of worrying about the setbacks you might face, consider how you might learn and grow from them.

# INSIGHTS

The connecting thread here is important: you don't need to stay on track to succeed. That football player who could have been anything? Perhaps they focused on being the best partner they could ever be. That young basketballer who 'dropped out' at 19 might now have a doctorate in design, because he learned at a young age the power of making difficult decisions, and the power to stop what you are good at to pursue what you want.

Your worth is not defined by what you achieve or acquire, but by who you become and how you contribute to the world.

Self-esteem should come from character, not success or status. The highest accomplishment is to be a person of generosity, curiosity, humility and integrity.

In my journey in cricket and life, I discovered the destination isn't important. What is important is the journey, the moments of learning and the experiences that shape us. As well as a sport, junior cricket was a lesson in resilience, teamwork and understanding my limits and potential. It was a playground where I could experiment, fail and succeed—all without the pressure of an end goal. This freedom to explore and grow ultimately prepared me for the realities of adult life. The only end goals I ever heard of were from adults, often who fell short of their own making.

Of course, knowledge and learning come with the challenge of transforming that knowledge into action. Gathering information and becoming aware of what must be done is easy. But bridging that gap—consistently applying what you've learned—is where actual growth happens, and this is a little more complicated. You need to make daily conscious decisions to align your actions with our values and goals.

To move forward from cricket, I found reflecting on my past essential. Understanding where I came from, the lessons

*(continued)*

I learned and the experiences that shaped me gave me the clarity and strength to face the future. Sometimes, I make peace with things that don't make sense, while working to better understand the things that do. However, I've also realised that life isn't just about reflecting on the past or planning for the future. It's about being present, embracing the now and making the most of every moment.

Early in my career, I would build brands or create ideas. When it got hard, I got stuck. I would explore ways to simplify the problem, but I feared the pressure and how hard it got. Over time, I started to learn that I had created that pressure, and I knew that the pressure of never starting was far less painful than the pressure of starting and failing.

Now let's drill into another question adults like to throw around: 'What's the worst that could happen?' Sure, it seems like a simple question. But when my 'worst' came, it wasn't simple at all. This hurt me for years to come.

The worst moment in my business life came after one of my first businesses collapsed in 2003. At the time our business was factoring our invoices with a debtor finance company in Sydney—a legitimate and clever way to finance a business. (Invoice factoring is a line of credit that helps you turn your outstanding customer invoices into a source of readily available funding.) When we closed the company, however, the invoice factoring company wanted their money paid back immediately. I agreed to go into the office in Sydney and sit with the accounts receivables manager. I was stressed, unwell and in the process of winding up a company—with 30 staff, five company cars, shops and offices—at the age of 29. It was a nightmare experience, but the worst came from the finance company.

I sat next to the accounts manager as he made phone calls to my current clients and other businesses, as well as old clients of mine with whom I had spent years building relationships. He would tell them, with me present, that I had gone broke and they now owed him (the finance company) money. It was awful; he made me feel like a criminal, and like working to build something that provided jobs and opportunities for people—and then failing—was pathetic. He, on the other hand, chasing the money I had lost, was almighty and empowered. He talked down to me, his tone seeming to imply I had stolen from him.

The offices were messy, smelly and had no windows. The desks were cluttered and tight, and the staff looked tired. He looked exhausted and scruffy. He had wispy hair, thick glasses and an English accent, and he would put the phone down to my customers and say things like, 'Well, I bet she was a right bitch, aye' or 'We'll get that money off that prick, don't worry'.

Every 30 minutes or so, he would go downstairs and out into a nearby alley for a smoke, and I had to go with him because I had no security to stay in the building. We would stand in the back alley as he smoked, and he would ask me questions about women and girls and fashion. We spent eight hours together that day in his cubicle, his little corner box that felt suffocating; it was the only real time in my life that I wanted to smash someone's face in, quite literally. By the time 5 pm rolled around, I would have been happy if his smug face was buried in his giant grey box computer monitor with a cigarette, lit, stuffed up his ass. He was disgusting — the environment, the people, the way I was treated and the way he treated people was like nothing I had experienced. I swore I would never do business with the company again — and I haven't.

I hated that day more than any other in my business life. But it taught me about integrity. It taught me about the kind of business I wanted to be and reminded me that, while that was bad, I got to go home to my wife and Miff, who was almost one. We need those days to ensure the good days are worth it. Without the yin, we get no yang. While that day — and many more since — was terrible, I'm still here; I got back up and kept moving forward. I often think about that guy, wondering what he is doing.

You know, the only worse feeling than a day as dark as that is not trusting yourself to start something again after — to believe that you can't or are not good enough. You can't let other people steal your confidence or belief that whatever you're going through will only make you stronger. Because it will, and it does.

## INSIGHTS

On reflection, I realise the business I had to close in 2003 gave me four years of joy leading up to that day. Why should that one bad experience deter me from experiencing the four years of creation and opportunity? It shouldn't, and it doesn't.

*(continued)*

I often think back to that night at the Dolce & Gabbana restaurant in Milan that I talk about back in chapter 5. Impostor syndrome is not a clue that you're unqualified or not good enough. It's a sign of hidden potential. When you think others overestimate you, you're more likely to underestimate yourself.

I don't know why you bought this book or read this far, but I have an inkling it was because you have had something lying dormant in the back of your mind for a long time. Maybe at some point, someone or something said you couldn't. It's easy to find reasons why we can't, but maybe it is time to look for the one reason why we should.

Brené Brown says, 'Courage starts with showing up and letting ourselves be seen'. Show people your dreams, talk about your ideas and unleash them!

For months before and after that incident with the invoice factoring company, I was down and out about my business's public failure. I had withdrawn, steering clear of friends and family. I was broken.

Early one Sunday morning just after Christmas of that year, a text arrived from one of my closest lifelong friends, Josh Evans. Josh and his wife, Laura Demasi, have supported my business ventures and offered unwavering friendship without judgement. That summer, he knew that my business was gone, and I was in pain.

The message said: 'Bondi Beach, swim, 10 am, then coffee with the fam.'

Miff was a baby and Laura was pregnant, expecting their first boy, Orlando.

My initial response was typical for that period. 'Nah, busy today, can't make it.'

Nicola, who'd also received the text, countered with, 'Yeah, we can make it. See you at 10 am!'

This straightforward invitation was the catalyst for a day of profound transformation and a turning point in my life.

I messaged, 'Can we meet at the beach, the north end? I'm not up for seeing anyone or bumping into someone I might know'. We used to own a retail store in Bondi and I knew our old staff members lived there or nearby. And because we worked in fashion, everyone I had ever employed outside of the Bondi store also lived in the area, including Josh and Laura.

So we met at the north end of Bondi, where I had hoped to blend into the background and somehow find a secluded spot on the bustling Bondi Beach — an impossible feat. Sensing my discomfort, Josh suggested, 'Let's swim out towards the rocks and around the headland'. I thought, *No-one out there, void of people. Brilliant plan.* 'I am in!'

As I have mentioned throughout this book, the ocean is my sanctuary. It's a place where the notifications, pings and buzzes of the modern world can't find us. This need for a refuge is the reason I have never owned an Apple watch. I sometimes don't need to be contacted, and this was one of those mornings.

As we swam out to sea, the beach in the background faded, the people got smaller, and I felt stronger. I was in nature, and after months of feeling down, I felt strong. This was what I needed: a moment in nature, void of people and questions.

Josh and I were treading water about 600 metres off the shore, talking about kids and life, when I heard a familiar voice cutting through the vastness. 'Ben Rennie, is that you?'

It was Amanda, an old friend and business colleague, swimming past us. She had glimpsed my bald head, bobbing away in the water out to sea, and somehow recognised it.

'Wow, amazing, what a coincidence! I can't believe I'm bumping into you out here; oh, Ben, I am so sorry to hear about your business!', she said.

Josh's face went blank; he looked stunned. I was a little shocked, too. Here I was face to face with the very thing I wanted to avoid, the reason we had swum out to sea. Then Amanda's friend arrived a minute later — Darryn Lyons, one of the world's most famous paparazzi photographers. Shooting the stars through his photography empire, he had established a name for himself in London in the 1990s. He gained widespread media attention when his company sold a photograph to the *News of the World*, which was used to support a claim that football star David Beckham was having an affair with his assistant Rebecca Loos.

On the night of the fatal car crash involving Princess Diana in 1997, Darryn's company, Big Picture, received photographs of Diana's final moments. Darryn still owns these photos — they have never been published, and he has vowed to never sell them.

Darryn has a distinctive presence and, that day out at sea, I knew who he was but had never met him. He looked at me and said in his ever-present Australian accent, 'Hey mate, how are you? What's happening?'

Amanda replied, 'Oh, Ben owned the Australia distribution rights for Boxfresh, but his company is being wound up and closed down. Do you know Boxfresh, Darren?'

I sank further, wishing a shark could pull me under! In this moment, I felt like being swallowed whole by a humpback whale would somehow feel more comfortable than the conversation I was having with Darryn and Amanda.

Darryn's reply would change my perspective on life. It went something like this: 'Ah fuck, fuck me, well that's fucked. Fucking hell, hey; how are you holding up?'

Treading water, just, I replied, 'Not good, Darryn, it's been tough'!

His reply: 'Look where we are; look at what we are doing. The sun is shining, the water is warm, and this shit is free, nature is free. Look back at that beach — you will find doctors, lawyers, backpackers, designers, surfers, wankers, assholes, good people and kind people. There is a common thread: we all share a beach today, mate. It's not bloody hard. Life doesn't need to be so complicated. The best things in life are free, so at least enjoy that today and chin up. Tomorrow brings a new day... tomorrow is always a new day!'

I remember that reply word for word. He was right. With a nod, Darryn and Amanda pushed on. Josh gave me a knowing, relieved look of, 'Oh, wow' as we swam over to the rocks.

As I walked back to the sand, Nicola, Laura and Miffy were waiting on towels. 'Wow, Ben', Nicola said, 'you look like you have grown six inches!'

## INSIGHTS

We can't escape our past, but we can remember this: the things we think will break us are often what make us. For me, after my company failed, I had been at home wallowing and wondering how to save myself, where to go and what to do next. The day after my swim and chat with Darryn, I hit the newspapers and searched the job ads, looking for a way to rebuild. And within four weeks, I was the new sales and marketing director for Luxottica, the world's largest eyewear company. This role would take me around the world and connect me with some of the most critical people I have ever met. It would lead me to design, where I feel most at home.

We cannot connect the dots looking forward; we can only connect them looking back. Be bold and look back occasionally but, more importantly, remember that moving forward gives us the stories to look back on.

Most of what you worry about will not happen, but I guarantee that a few things you dreamed about will.

Share your ideas, and if you need a sounding board, I'm here to listen. Your voice matters.

I often hear people say, 'I had this idea, but someone has already done it'.

If something has already been done before (and, let's face it, most things have), you should do it again. The concept of competition is irrelevant. Creative work is unique and personal. Each thing you create can only ever reflect your individual experiences, perspectives and vision. Comparing yourself to others can be counterproductive, distracting you from your true path.

**Each of us has an irreplaceable perspective. Embracing your uniqueness is the key to creating authentic and meaningful work.**

Your goal is not to compete with others but to express your unique voice. Each of us has an irreplaceable perspective. Embracing your uniqueness is the key to creating authentic and meaningful work. Your work is yours, and that's what makes it special.

By letting go of the notion of competition, you can free yourself from unnecessary pressures. This liberation allows you to focus on your journey, growth and exploration. Other creators are not your rivals but sources of inspiration, pushing you to delve deeper into your creative reservoir.

Every human is a unique storyteller with a voice that deserves to be heard. Your uniqueness is your journey. I guarantee it's worth sharing. I shared mine, and look where that landed — right into your hands.

Start where you are, use what you have and create something unique that you can bring to the world.

# INSIGHTS

When my daughter Miff was born, Nicola and I painted a mural above her cot featuring the final words from *The House at Pooh Corner*. It reminded us that while parenthood carries its profound moments, it's also about play, dreams and joy. The mural read:

> *So, they went off together. But wherever they go, and whatever happens to them on the way, in that enchanted place on the top of the forest, a little boy and his Bear will always be playing.*

This was a message for our daughter, but also for us—a reminder to never let go of that playful spirit. When we sold our house, the family who moved in chose to keep the mural—a testament to the lasting power of its sentiment.

Your past is part of you, woven from joy, heartache, lessons and the dreams that have shaped who you are. It can't be erased, but it doesn't need to limit your future. Each day is a blank canvas, ready to be filled with new ideas, experiences and possibilities.

Too often, we exchange playfulness for the grind of adulthood—overwhelmed by goals, duties and the pressure to prove our worth. But here's the truth: you don't have to justify your existence. Life is not just about achievements; it's about living fully, connecting deeply and creating meaning.

So, take a moment. Reconnect with that 'enchanted place' inside you—the part that still believes, dreams and finds joy in the simple things. Let your past fuel you, but allow each day to be a fresh chance to embrace creativity with wonder.

Wherever you go and whatever happens to you along the way, in your enchanted place on top of your own forest, I hope you and yours will always be creating.

# CONCLUSION:
# MY ENDING IS YOUR BEGINNING

Creativity is a journey—a process of reimagining, exploring and finding the courage to start again (and again). Uncovering your creative confidence can transform how you see the world and how the world sees you.

Creativity is playful, fearless and unbound by rules. It asks you to trust yourself and to take action even in the face of adversity. Each small step builds creative confidence and pushes your fears aside.

Your past may shape your journey, but the present offers a fresh canvas to create something uniquely yours.

Whether it's a sketch on a napkin, a bold business idea or a simple shift in perspective, your creativity can reshape your life and change the world around you in ways you may never expect. (And I promise it will take you to the places you once dreamed about.)

Thank you for sharing this journey with me. Writing this book has been my most creative adventure; knowing you got this far means everything.

I'd love to hear your story—what you've created, where your creativity has taken you and what inspires you to keep going. Share your journey with me at benrennie.com. I can't wait to hear from you.

The world needs your ideas, dreams and courage.

Thank you.

**Ben Rennie**

# ACKNOWLEDGEMENTS

Everything I've ever learned is borrowed. Nothing is original. Every idea, every belief, and every creative instinct reflects the people I know, love, and trust. This book is no different — it belongs to my community.

It has been shaped in early morning surfs, mid-morning breakfasts, and late-night conversations over barbecues with friends (you know who you are). I've always said the answers are out there, not in here — but because of you, my friends who are out there, you now live inside here ♥.

This book simply would not have been written without the unwavering support of my friend **Luke Shanahan** — the most creative human I have ever met. His belief in me, his relentless encouragement, and his ability to see things others don't have shaped this book and how I think about creativity. Luke, your influence runs through these pages in more ways than I can count. Thank you.

**To Nicola**

For always letting me dream. For never once asking me to be anything other than who I am. For catching me when I fall, no matter how high I jump. I hope I've done the same for you.

**To Miff**

You dream big and never settle. Watching you pursue your passion has made me braver in pursuing mine.

**To Kai**

You are fearless in your expression, which is the purest form of creativity. Never stop singing your song.

### To Pip

For always speaking your truth, never compromising, and creating for the sake of creating. You remind me that art should never ask for permission.

### To Mum

You made me believe I could do anything, and that belief became the foundation for everything.

### To Dad

For teaching me that strength and vulnerability can exist in the same breath. For showing me that it's okay for a man to cry. And for all the hours you spent bowling to me until you couldn't anymore — thank you. You were Mum's hero, and you're mine too.

### To My Family

Minnie, Cooper, Meghan, Xavier, and your beautiful mums, Tracey, Cody, and Chrissie, are the strongest people I know. Your light is impossible to miss. Jack and Emily Hogarth, McKenzie and Ainsley Stone — I've watched you grow into brilliant, ambitious, creative humans, and I couldn't be prouder.

### To My Inner Circle

Jason Stone, Adam Webb, Simon Williams, Ben Taylor, Glenn and Rebecca Chandler, Em and Liam Chandler, Michaela Vlazney, Josie Kelley, Clare and Dave Hogarth, Lucy Rose, Luke Shanahan, and Chance Burns, your friendship has been my foundation. You've never let me stop trying.

### To My Business Partners

Paul Breen, Andrew Fallshaw, Jason Stone, Steve Fisher, Tony Morrissey, Glen Barry, Ben Johnston, Anna Robertson, Glenn Chandler, Austin Smidt, Andrew Robertson, Leigh Stokes, and Andrew Simpson, thank you for your trust, shared vision, and pursuit of something better.

### To My Community

For every hand you lent, every spare $100 given when I needed it, every couch offered, every message sent at the right time — you've shaped me more than you know.

To Stacey, Luke and Willow Dalton, Andy & Michelle Massey, Chris Farmer, Luke Shanahan, Tim Ross, Willo, Gordon Campbell, Leigh Bailey, Irish Mick, Jane and Matt Park, Choco, Charlotte Reid, Anthony Kelly, Josh Evans, Tim Ross, Dave and Liza Kelly, Dave Winner, Lote Tuqiri, Scott Penrose, Darren Pedemont and Wazza, Aaron Curnow,

Pete McGrath, Peter Jordan, Adam Luck, Chris Norman, Gavin Bostik, Dave Tanner, Ian Pepper, Johnny Highland, Kevin Thompson, Steve Winner, Ed Melina, Steve Aggers, Ace Selijaas, Gary Selijaas, Garry Sheen, Tara Gorman, Shannon and Stuart Karpinnen, The Waughs, Andrew Grant, Vashti Whitfield, Kate Dawson, Gus Dawson, Tom Dawson, Marg Dawson, Meg Dawson, Anna Dawson, Chris Dawson, Rik Dawson, Brent Dawson, Tim Dawson, Pap and Gran, Nan and Pop, Lorraine Carter, Peter Carter, Christine Carter, Chip Liedel, Rhonda Brighton Hill, Shara Reid, Ellidy Pullin, Rik Guselli, Kristine Guselli, Courtney van der Weyden, Jen Hampton (Hayden), Dave Winner, Leon Tarbotton, Mikey Williams, Chance Burns, Austin Smidt, Liz and Ken Stone, The Utah Prep Family, Tamsin & Marco Maunder, Shelly & Rod Morgan — your impact on my life has been immeasurable.

To Everyone Who Ever Supported or Bought From Boxfresh, Iota, Standard, Monocle, Reny, Hops & Craft, Vinology, Vert, Utopia, Royal, Stone Island, CP Company, 6.2 — you were part of the journey, and I am endlessly grateful.

To Those Who Invited Me Into the Circle to Build a Better World: To the incredible teams at Surfrider, Chumpy Pullin Foundation, Design Declares, Heart Foundation, Skin Check Champions, Cancer Council, Indigenous Marathon Foundation, B Corp, B Corp Climate Collective, Protect Our Winters, 1% for the Planet, and Clean Creatives — thank you for the work you do and for letting me be part of it.

Please continue to support these causes:

🌱 For design in business → designdeclares.com.au

🌏 For climate action → surfrider.org.au

**And Finally...**

To the Wiley Publishing Australia team, particularly Lucy Raymond, for trusting in my writing and helping bring this book to life — thank you.

*Not everyone who shaped me is on these pages for the right reasons. Some lessons came the hard way, through difficult relationships and moments of reckoning. But as I've always believed, creativity — and life — is just as much about what we take forward as what we choose to leave behind.*

Love & Create.